a year from today

Stacy Szymaszek   a year from today

NIGHTBOAT BOOKS
NEW YORK

ISBN 978-1-937658-76-2

Design and typesetting by Margaret Tedesco
Text set in Futura and Century Schoolbook
Cover photograph by Stacy Szymaszek

Cataloging-in-publication data is available
from the Library of Congress

Nightboat Books
New York
www.nightboat.org

This book was written from April 2014 to April 2015. It concludes a trilogy of poetic journals (*hart island, Journal of Ugly Sites and Other Journals*) that I began in 2008. Each one became more autobiographical, and therefore uncomfortable. What if I publically declared (did not exclude, nor confess) the particulars of my day-to-day struggles, formally, in writing? How long could I sustain an autobiography in verse? Could the process of aestheticizing experience be a route to deeper self-knowledge and transformation (for myself, for a reader?) These were the risks I charged myself with. Reading this text 3 years later is similar to the temporal confusion of walking down 2nd Avenue remembering all the places I used to frequent that no longer exist. Another risk with "life-writing" is that things change. I am no longer married, some friendships documented in this book didn't stand the test of time either, and as I write this, I am in the process of concluding my 11-year tenure as Director of The Poetry Project—a locality that holds these journal books together, work born of work.

—SS

SPRING

       goblet of   Spanish wine
engulfs my face   I'm late   chair next to Anne is empty   she opens
more than one scarf   spring starts with Anne's birthday
"Aren't you cold?" my blazer is
blue and gray wool   scarf is from
Dress Shoppe II   made in India 1908
later it falls from her   she calls   I trace her steps

find it

"I FUCKING FOUND IT"
                  "YOU FUCKING FOUND IT"

                         on steps of a brownstone on 10th

it's that shop on 2nd with yellow trim

left my address on a postcard   proprietor
said   "for a love note"

                              * * *

Simone and I split cost of quince branches
Amiri Baraka Tribute Oliver Lake
           Matthew Shipp

listening to their records today with   half the branches in a tinted
blue jar

"I dig the way language changes
                  it changes
                  so quickly too…"
went to Tsampa
cool and soft   this was hard
Julie   "can you take a sabbatical?"   I look up "sabbatical"
biblically   a ceasing
                  in the seventh year

"just kicking it   subtext   not doing shit"   (Lake)

* * *

I have a soft spot
for fuck-ups
                  i.e. the new pup
sleeping by my side
                        restless in my   saint-
            to-the-animals   robe   I move into my rising sign
      time to hit   the road
            visit to Gail in Montréal on hold

truth is   I can't figure out how
to get out of here

* * *

I look forward to one moveable feast
HOLY WEEK   OFF   church celebrates Easter
I celebrate the dawn goddess
                         and dream of slaying dragons   it is writ ARTS
BE GONE   you are not
HOLY   eat   one
ritual meal

kielbasa   scrambled eggs   black coffee from a kettle   side of horsey

MAKE ART

* * *

Fish Fry isn't
                a thing here
my mom
                         describes Friday

        "I scraped off the batter
        I ate the perch
        it's mostly batter"

        I describe my meal   she tells me the plot

                              of an episode   "did you see it?"

refuses to remember that I don't have a TV   too weird
she has 3   set to the same channel

surround sound   means   surrounded by sound

                              *   *   *

group email from a young poet
list of readings he's excited about

do people ever feel their age?
why is this child behind my eyes
when I've grown this old?

Charles said I was wise
to recognize that the young have to decide
who among their peers
gets recognized   I'm in the   catbird's seat?
                    more like   the crow's nest

       THERE'S 20 PEOPLE ON THAT BILL

let's say it's a Midwest   ethos
more tugboat less showboat

* * *

don't winter well   any-
more   losing my Wis-
consin   Julie says this winter
the wind blew ex-
tra holes in
the milk

* * *

open front door first thought   someone is burning

                          frankincense

from my fourth floor window I can see downtown
Brooklyn   through smoke

no sirens   and the day
                              particularly quiet
still a chill and
gray
          perfect for taking pictures
do I wash my hair?   no

brush the dog   his white fur blows

through the empty branches
                                        front room   buds
on quince branch
transferred to coffee can   flower

                                    * * *

Kostas sends me a link   feeling sure   I would already
know but I don't
                        about "8 Poems for Ninetto" trans. by Peter Valente
Pasolini nudge
my excuses   I have to go to ROME   OSTIA
                        have to learn some ITALIAN   translate ROMAN POEMS MY-
SELF   READ MORE   UNDERSTAND MORE   when is my
Mystical Experience?   but I do know   "insane with grief"
when a soon to be ex-lover assures   "nothing will change"

REWRITE PASOLINI POEMS   at the age he was when he died
if I am lost he will find me   like when he cast Ninetto as

        Aziz   in Arabian Nights   "joy   happiness   a living ballet"

* * *

smoke was a brush fire in Jersey
much warmer today   I'm not great
at not working   and I'm great
at procrastinating
               hold that paradox
I'm not great at routine   taking my pills
everyday   going to bed at a regular
time   or starting work at the same time
         everyday   I'm reliable
but sometimes I'm hard to reach in my own
world because it's truly great
               in   there   many emails to respond
to   and send   twilight life
shocked open at 3am

* * *

much warmer today   row of empty iced tea bottles
curb-side   dog pees on them
I'm giving him too much
lead   as usual   at vet   look up to see skylight   the roof
where the last dog   ate donuts   cheese   and   cat
food before they   stopped her heart
         I talk about her to the receptionist

without feeling too sad   Dr. Faigle
her otherworld guide   just had a chubby baby
we all hope she comes back   to meet
this new guy   his problem ears   his fear   vet techs say
"uh oh"   but when
unmuzzled   he's all kisses
                forgiveness and forgetfulness or
                        we just   roll with it

* * *

exciting when the automated
                        voice   says   next
                                stop 2nd Avenue   Edwin
                                        Denby   says
it's so exhausting
                to keep looking   it's self-
                                preservation to just look
a little   I forget   what I see
without my notebook
                        three good-looking teen boys   speaking Spanish
                                one basketball   one crucifix necklace
everyone's looking at their phones   I do it too   just not
today   woman in brown leather trench   very short
                skirt   leg poised outward   reading
                        In Cold Blood   hardcover
on the avenue I smell

an orange   man is leaning over   so he doesn't dribble
everyone pretending
         it's warmer than it is
outdoor dining   because it's April 10
    and there are no buds
           on the trees   stop at East Village Books
         do what I do   haunt the religion section
find four   including St. Augustine's   *Confessions*   cash
only? I'll get cash   hold on...
   while I'm gone   his colleague shelves my books
you're too efficient I say   with a smile
    he feels criticized   oh well

orthodox kid asking passersby   "are you Jewish?"   skips me
     erica told me about
          Mitzvah tanks   they have cookies   the HRC kids
never skipped me   asking if I had a moment
for gay marriage

    where are they now
      and what do they ask
        people on the street?

fleet of apple green cabs   imagine
all the meetings to settle on that color

returned to a store where a queen sold
me a flannel   tending to my gender
it's boarded up

first in a series of four   blood moons   maybe
I'll catch the other
three

"it's hard when you're different
sizes different places   even me   my hips"
he said

NO BROOKLYN BOUND F TRAINS

so uptown to W. 4th   train waiting with open doors   hop on   it's the D   why did I get on?
it was there   get off at 34th St.   transfer to F   woman on down escalator doesn't move as I
charge up behind her   I imagine sliding down the rail but instead miss the train
somehow we agree to civil order   this F goes to Brooklyn   2 men asleep on the love seat

the rest of us have dark glasses as the sun is out so infrequently we are ever ready for it to blaze upon our subterranean faces   train turns into an A   digital sign says pay attention to the crew   he speaks into a voice scrambler   a woman with a kid asks me what's going on   a man with part of his ear growing out of his cheek says he just moved here and needs to get I don't remember where   I explain this train is rogue but I'm sticking with it   wherever it takes me   as long as it's over the East River

* * *

bedroom has a door and a balcony
one April night it got a little muggy
so I opened the door   the sounds
of downtown Brooklyn were shoved
down into the earth by singing birds
huh   all along the city was an aviary
or a murder mystery   I'll always go mystical
St. Francis over Hitchcock   but will befriend
a crow over a sparrow   or a lark   resonate
with a caw over a coo or chirp   it was like
Buckminster Fuller's geodesic dome encasing
Boerum Hill   making echoic birds

* * *

I've put on some pounds after   losing some
dark circles   under my eyes   are darker

you have to wonder   at this age   when the body slips
will it   "become again   very strong?"   (Simone)

decade plus age difference   I don't need the same sleep

                    in my best position my arm aches   and vague
                    worries wake me   most nights

        oatmeal   dog at my feet   last night

I visited Gail   in Montréal   in truth

            my passport has never been   used   is in a wooden cabinet
with expired licenses   outdoor furniture covered in ice

                    K breaking a fever
                    dog with ulcerated ears   "angry"   says the British vet

attempt to drip steroids   pay
bills for my eyes and teeth   parts exempt from coverage

what a house of maladies   no one liked that picture

I look good in blue

Rachel says "my god you answered"   it's a Good Friday miracle

it's fine you kissed her   it's fine

you missed the reading   I got hurt

maybe we seem mean when we're hurt   baby it was cold

in flannel cardigan and denim   Paul and Matt held me close

A MANWICH

to keep me warm   asking the men in my life to do

what my daddy never did   a little compassion

for the gender metronome   vs.   my irregular timing

don't argue when I say I'm on the verge

of obscurity   within a wider irrelevance   it's part of being with the central office

so central but

like pork belly

what happens to the other parts?

O SOLE MIO   O SOTTOVOCE   and then

there was John

hugs "Italian style"   man-saints   see me

thru Aries

vague worries   my natural enemy   the wind

* * *

ring of kielbasa   scrambled eggs   and kraut   about
the only familial meal I make Easter   after Easter
but the meat is turkey meat   do you have a
                                                bonnet?

I don't respond to *bonnet*   dog watches from office

        tomorrow is Monday a far cry from Maundy
return to hellhole   nail in window   as little devils hang
                                                off scaffolding

upping the dandy ante   new orange ascot

        he added 10 more performers then had a breakdown   or vice versa?
cc'd women to cover   it's that emotional
sipping fresh almond milk with turmeric
                                    at a table that has been in the family
for generations   asked my parents   am I obliged to keep it?
because I don't want this table   they said
it's an antique   call a dealer   load the
                                lineage onto a truck
as I turn to embrace Danish
                    Modern   trace the ants from the bottle   of Pinot
Noir all the way to the crack in the back
                        door   through a mountain village
                        of books   try to slow time

by piecing together their

       mysterious work   watch a movie   the kind
I would have quoted a lot   if I had seen it
in high school   remember the day when I presented my class
scenes from *The Dead Zone* on career day   my ambition
     to become a parapsychologist   somewhat related to
the results of   a standardized test   everything niche
             getting older contemplating
              if I'm too old
                to change

         * * *

read an *Al-Jazeera* article   the old   "poetry
          is dead" thing   how much

social acceptability   do I need

this haircut?   I told the stylist
          make it more gay
more important to distinguish
       these things   because lets face
it we fall in and out
     of favor   hatred repeats itself

a pleasure system   as Sarah says
       of homophobia

Easter is over
and my work   is not fulfilled

I can't pass
              through closed doors   I've discovered the weak

spots of villains and they progress in their
                                        autonomy

                         * * *

maybe the way to go about this
is to stay within earshot   and sip the Wild Turk.

        "Hustlers of the world, there is one Mark you cannot beat: The Mark Inside."
                                                    (Burroughs)

musician asks for payment to read a few moments amongst poets not getting
        paid and gets paid

                        see a woman asking for spare change I'm holding
        coffee with honey   make a point
            of speaking   vs. averting   only to say

                        don't think I have any

"ladies and gentlemen I'm one of New York's homeless ladies..."

guy at the shop where I get coffee is from my hometown
saw my tote bag and said he loves that place

"I mean no disrespect..."

said he's my fan   "you always get a small"

now I go in there
WHERE IS MY FAN?

THE PERSONAL IS PERSONA   what else should I tell him?

"Cheat your landlord if you can and must..."   (Burroughs)

usually don't take honey   I have some honey is all

people want to perform earlier so they can split   get it   get it   but it doesn't
make for much of a celebration

me and a pack
``````of chewing gum``````
``````````````````````````````````
``````````````````````````````````
``````````````````````````````````

some women don't worry about the ramifications of
their anger
                         possession is nine-tenths   of the law

I look deep in the mirror   and watch my lips move silently
                         imitating the priest
                         "get.
                         the.
                         fuck.
                         off.
                         this.
                         property."

                    * * *

dream   :   I purchase three notebooks
they are sage   one of them
has a fastener   I guess   for the secrets I keep
         people are sharing pictures of cherry blossom trees   it has been
brutal waiting for this moment
                         as soon as my IRS deposit came through
              purchased a Vitamix and renter's insurance
rest will just pay rent   I've killed many ants   with nontoxic citrus spray

I'm too bitter   bathe the dog   dry him like a baby   but this one is less like a baby
than the others
              interpret the notebooks

as needing to be more open to seeing   I'm such a Cancer
in my own mansion   had plans   I was excited about   but not as excited
as when I cancelled

                        tonight   watched "Crimes of the Century"
                        feel empathy   for none   other than
                        the Unabomber   who thought it insensitive that his cabin

was exhibited in a museum   who was turned in by his brother after reading his manifesto
in the *Times*   recognized his style   the '90s crimes   I scarcely remember   their impact
my withdrawn '90s   Ted Kaczynski   the end of being able
to mail a package in a mailbox

                                        * * *

spring gleaning   vs.   spring cleaning
never stop acquiring books
evaluate every title
                      after 15 years of lugging it
going to part with Kenner's *The Pound Era*   now 100% sure
I will never read it
                      pull out Rexroth's mountain writings
which I got on Sunset Boulevard
                      I'd like to be in L.A.
                      or on a mountain

* * *

she wanted breakfast for a change   ate one turkey bacon wrapped the other in foil
for the road   woke up at 5am   killed more ants   yesterday with a tissue
escorted a bee out the door   bettered insect karma   yesterday I bought
nuts   clerk had gloves with fingers cut off   we just have to accept
April as part of winter now   stopped in front of the Polish
G.I. to see the pastries NO! I don't do that anymore   now 8am
the light has minimally changed   bracing through storm   siren setting
the dog off   the most horrible howl   breaking into screeching
not sonorous at all   thought this was akin to communing
with a pitch but now I wonder   if it pains him   looked for a great Italian
dictionary to teach myself to translate   that's what's missing from my practice
"let's do something coupley"   "like what   play a game?" thinking of
Lewis F's ethics of reading   found a Whalen book   in the office
Michael Goldberg's copy   open to a poem for Rexroth
"Weather Odes" and in Rexroth open to a poem "Spring Rain"   it rains
and rains   I'm not one of those people who complains in August   trained myself
to believe that I will retire to New Mexico   see Southwest patterns
in my mind's eye   K says no wind chimes   and why do I
complain so much   I do?   shit   don't know what I mean by coupley
rearrange things?   it is NOW/ that I must…make /That move that will
be the foundation/For that spectacular success which must illuminate /All my
later days" (Whalen)   I live a circumspect life in some ways   direct
effects of homophobes obscured   don't look for who's really
in charge   c'est moi!   to those who were and will be horrible

to my brother I do and will not like you   will no longer help you
yet it's hard to stepoff the high road   when I smell smoke I won't mention
your names to friends   just hope you are smudging out the nastiness inside
"the treetops/vanish in fog" (Rexroth) Tuesday had the deficit feel
of Thursday and today has the laze of a Friday went nuts
on the cheese after the reading   exchanged cards with a T. McBee
made a plan to have lunch with James "do you like to eat?" what a strange
question   James says I would be surprised by how many people in our community
don't like to experience pleasure when you put it that way   decides Emporio
endorsed by Roman friends   I'm not surprised   pleasure can be confusing
can feel like my vigilance is slacking   but I do like to eat   it's May
Day   I go to the distress signal in voice procedure said three times but
it's May Day two words meaning International Workers' Day   stemming
from the pre-Christian holiday of Beltane a celebration of rebirth
it's quite common for a New Yorker to work 10 to 15 hour days
I can't do that even for poetry   writing this at the tail end of a
flash flood MAKE YOUR DEMAND FOR SIX HOURS
I mean   lets think more about Epicurus "ally comrade"
freedom from fear   absence of pain   surrounded by friends events
based on the motions and interactions of atoms moving in empty space
his school was based in the garden of his house thus called   "The Garden"
when I can see downtown again I will stand on the balcony   imagine
summer pastures   imagine how I have to imagine cows now

* * *

from down ½ block   saw a man staring
at what I thought was a toy
                              shock of red
on the pavement
was chest of what I now know to be
          a Rose-breasted Grosbeak   male
                              upright   one wing spread

"a foliage gleaner"

          "rarely can be seen on the ground"

when I got there I stared too   eyes closed
no signs of life   but uncanny in position   upright

always worried about what
is right
          I decided
          not to move him   in case he was alive
to die untouched by a human
seemed right

* * *

watched Xavier Dolan movies back to back   a 44 year old
lesbian obsessed with a 25 year old man   life is sweet
and complex   I'm at the age where everyone young inspires the thought
"I could have given birth to you!" in 1989
the night I threw up Campari   but didn't have sex   my friends
put me to bed   cleaned up bright red streaks   my first experience of
alcohol excess   I'm proud of my film director son   his sartorial sense
his hair   replicated by my stylist from pictures I show her
but we both have mother issues   so if I was his mother his movie would be
about our conflict   I'm at the age where I feel that I have finally become
the high school kid I wanted to be   through mimicking the mannerisms
of those who are successful   and I lead with that   transmitting to the kid
knowledge that he's a late bloomer   there's a place called New York City
where he'll be part of a community   and he'll grow more
beautiful   in each movie there are scenes of tea time   close ups of the tea being
poured into 2 cups   sad things are happening
between 2 people who are close   who take a leap of faith in "tea time"
that ritual will smooth over aggression   and ease delusion

* * *

flashback in the bath this sea salt
soap   when I moved for love   stayed above a French
café in rural PA   the plot was French   with my lover

and the man who loved her   it dawned on me
in the bath   that I needed to move again
        not back   to where I came from
but ON   into a house in a city with unfamiliar people   to try
try again   the soap in the bath   claw foot   I remember well
        it was about to rain on an already muted pallet   everyone's love
a caul of dread
                    it smelled like this soap   that I buy
                        on Court St.   two bars   at a time   it has an anchor
            embossed on it   which the hair under my arms
            rubs away in one wash   the café owner's son's
                    name was the name of a famous fascist   after
I moved I still slept with my lover for a couple of years and other lovers
                    who were better for me

* * *

conflation of   Cinco de Mayo
with   Día de los Muertos

park of cherry blossoms   a shrine   briefly think

of the gone dog   this one jumps
                            on my lap
                            for the first time

baseball on gym TV
no CNN   so I watch the 14th inning
haven't followed the game

                                  since the Brewer's lost the World
Series in '82   still know the names of those guys
COOOOOP   mom thought was booing   crush
on Molitor   the mustache of Fingers

                                           boring

go grocery shopping   wander through   street
fair   Carroll Gardens carnival   WIN A GOLDFISH

and KING KONG SWING RIDE   roast corn and whole pigs   people
holding trees of cotton candy   slumped over in this
wind   the sun makes it seem like 2 days colliding

ethos of the street
carnival   doesn't feel safe   disguised
as a good time   read the thought crimes   of the attendants
                                        head home

give away theater books lined up on Warren   2 women
pass   "I told him 3 times   the script is derivative" don't notice the books
                if I were an agent and an actor   and actors wanted me
to represent them   and I got them parts   but stopped getting
the really juicy roles myself... oh hell   metaphors too pathetic
                    /// get a grip \\\

"You are a poet and a filmmaker. Is there a relation between these two roles?"
Pasolini: "As far as I'm concerned, there is a profound unity between the two of them."

              dream :   performer with deformed mouth
                      sends me out to get peanuts

try not to text while walking   fear of falling
                                  into open
                                manholes   walked
in front of an ambling bus
                        passenger yelled
                        "how stupid are you?"
a familiar voice

            several years ago
            I didn't understand
            why people text   now
                          I pull over
                          to the shoulder
it's anxiety
            Zorba's "full catastrophe"

WHAT IF SOMEONE NEEDS ME and CAN'T FIND ME

                        it's my responsibility
                        born to be wild   no   born

to stand sentinel

in Milwaukee

                there's a grocery chain called Sentry

they guard your food

till you need more

                        * * *

CRANE MELVILLE STEIN sandwich   tips of my wingtips

touch   stone   "permit me voyage" (Crane)   "sometimes

            I am permitted…" (Duncan)   huh. permits

Xu Bing's Phoenix installation at St. John's   stomachs are dump

trucks   bird call that we heard

           during the meeting   what

was it?   PHIL   the white peacock   missed my stop up here   reading

another PHIL   Whalen and the day before   too absorbed writing

a grocery list   Eileen : have time for a coffee?   HUNGARIAN PASTRY SHOP

                   me : yes   blazers off   butterflies

                        * * *

"now that we have daybreak"   the basket and the balloon

separated   CNN talks to an expert in New Mexico   rest assured ballooning is safe   hit power line   exploded

tells the reporter   you know more about the story than I do

our vertical control is good   but horizontal   is up to the wind

recovery means 3 bodies   next story :   drone almost

hits passenger plane   unregulated drones!? drone hobbyists?!   woman

on commercial   sobbing at the bottom of her stairs   empty basket

spilled laundry   walking with K past a row

of basement apartments   warns me   at night these aren't

well lit   men who want to assault women look for this   in fact

a friend of a friend was   and didn't live   and no one was ever

caught   here we are not planning any vacations

that drone   came within 200 feet of a flight leaving NYC   lets

not go anywhere   ever   but that doesn't address   the balcony's

potential collapse   in the Great Lakes region   wild

rice is unable to grow in its traditional range   and in California…

well White House   in your state by state reports   there are 51 ways

to describe death by water   intense precipitation event   draught

fight against flames   mother nature will have us drinking

our own shit   such a paradoxical decade   the '60s

me   a glimmer   at the very end   no longer will children

outdo their parents   like the children of "the greatest

generation"   my elders in their 90s   steel worker   grade school math

teacher   bank teller   living frugally but well   me the ED

work or bust   no retirement   the environment

next story :   CNN reports Michael Sam was drafted   he's crying

on the phone   watching at the gym   threw the towel

over my head   gay news makes me cry   even as I wonder

if they would depict a straight football player in tears   or a straight white   football player   it's Mother's Day   many

pictures of cherry blossoms on the ground   harbinger of the

end of spring   if you follow the calendar   sent my mother

a bouquet called Big Love   on the morning show   girls give the female

reporters   single   roses   cultish   bad live music and mother

brunchers   I'm just trying to get in shape   don't have any

baby weight   just this sedentary lifestyle   genetically aged into a pear

shape   from the funniest thing my mother ever said about me

you're built like a brick shithouse   finally remember the Sunday farmer's

market   out of fresh eggs by 9am   bag my own   spinach   kale   asparagus

sign on the stinging nettles

"PROCEED WITH CAUTION—
USE TONGS"

* * *

Just sitting here watching the G go round
                              and round   ½ my writing day
                                                      shot
stand clear of the closing doors 3x   nothing
                                  derailment on   my mind
               weird vibe started
               last night
               at grocery store

don't want to "terminate" therapy   just quit   yet
I am a sucker for the restorative
like a process to end   when so many endings   are necessarily
abrupt   don't understand underwater tunnels or that my body

shoots through them 5 days a week   "we're restoring the Montague
                                                        tubes"
there's that word again   "we're flood proofing downtown"   MTA men
                                                      reflective vests
                                                      and gear
my lineage of builders   have come to terms

           with   "you got words"

* * *

hour and ½ uptown and back down
hour waiting
2 minutes to look at my   ovaries

                    the ownership
                    of cysts   a benign change

referral to an expert will get us closer to MRI approval   to rule it out 100%

but if you know it's benign... oh
                              this is about the system   thrown deep in
to rule it out
                there's that 1% uncertainty
if I have it
I could SUE
                she warns me

              the expert is a man   his protocol is

to have the woman insert the wand herself   "don't be freaked out"

what to do about these ovaries?   it's not like fibroids   no
                    shrinking up after menopause   they just hang out

threaten to change

have his number

haven't made the call   I want no hand

           in my demise   no   I want

               a butch angel to accompany me

               into the system

she has enormous breasts

a leather vest   she enters

the system with me   we bug them for my results   play gin while we're

on hold   argue with insurance reps   she would even

               insert the wand if I asked her to

*   *   *

All I ever wanted

All I ever needed

  riddling

    my head

all week

  never dug

    Depeche Mode

  what are those

next lines

words are

  very unnecessary

    they can only

do harm
    spin yarn how to
   roll out aspect
ratio chronic
   into chrono-
    meter perhaps
   this dispatch
becoming
too thick
  a dispatch
 too fast

             * * *

robin making a ruckus   perched
                    on flower box with flooded
  soil   no
  flowers   Ball jar with half lemon   spoon   stack of

novels   on the sill   4 squash
                  plants
                  came up   fled
                  the reading
       last night   watched history documentaries   on laptop
drifting in and out   hey Rosemary   the Kennedy I knew
because they secreted her   in my neck of
                  the woods

"this too shall pass"   dumbfounded
                    by certain emotions   as K is by tasks

            fixated on results   like
why would I write if I thought no one
                would read it   even my mom got at my diary   dad checked
my work   it's so clear
                            the day
                                    I paused   at the top of a hill
                                        on my bike   another stunt
                                        ending on my ass   now
the left side of my body is larger
I place the dog's tennis ball   in my armpit   let's call it

            accumulation   rock on
                    my chair   "sit on your perineum"

liver spot where hematoma was   magical realism
                                    is the worst   staggering home   nope
still don't look like someone
        you'd offer
                your seat to   all of my pockets
                                vibrating from one
                                            phone
                veer into bike
                    lane to avoid
                    the dark   passage

* * *

coast guard conducting   search and rescue
demonstration in the water
                    off of Coney Island   fleet week   feeling

        good in my body   balance

to "trouble in mind   I'm blue"   the Joplin

        version   Kostas gave me a bottle   of patchouli

smelled singular on him
as we hugged   on me
harkens to my hippie
                    emulation
                    period
                                    since I bought *The Tale of Genji*
                                        online book store notifies me
        of all tales

one way the 9/11 museum gift shop is   offensive   is
the unabashed admission
                    the best way to
                    honor
                        is to consume   I just learned

                        a poet   I used to hang out with
                        took his life   one of his   poems
online mourns
that everyone he knew   had been lost
to professionalism   should know better

than to start the day   with a documentary

          white police officer that disobeyed
          saved MOVE child   exiled by his police peers

          Birdie Africa the man   September 2013   drowned in a hot tub
                                                       on a ship at sea

                              *   *   *

                        observing   a dove
          cozy on the balcony   dog cozy on pillow   humans
staving off dread of a late afternoon Monday
                                              holiday
thin neck   K thinks sick   I think young
                                  my book   is out there
defer to bird space
now joined by another   mimetic bending motion of
                              our necks across the open

door   elder flies away
        younger has been   there a long time
               would it be so vigorously
               cleaning   if …

* * *

"PLOP PLOP FIZZ FIZZ"   what!
        run to the window   drunk guy singing   that was some jingle
           two summery days in a row   WHAT A RELIEF
      looking back is so
             I don't know   dog chewing my   sky blue no. 2

* * *

        when I met my friend   whose memorial
was this weekend   he had just sojourned to see Philip Whalen
       before he died   this was how I learned about   the poet Philip Whalen
who I spent the weekend reading   will share his work   with Naropa students
in June   at the time   I found it curious   men in the Midwest
      and their sojourns East or West   to dying poets   now
 I would prefer that   to go to the dying poet   instead
of them coming to me   we all ate
at a Japanese place   where Stephanie worked   no charge for the mochi   my
     friend so handsome   and young   left for

the Asian continent   his emails home
    scared me   made an error
    in distancing   as usual
when young   habits are hard to detect   when old   hard to break   he
"went manic"   oh   an error in degree of relatedness   <<<   people stop
    existing   blink   like a damn baby
       there was   trouble with the law   near Pueblo
    the law told him
    he couldn't go home

* * *

the test result service emails
auto-send at 4am   when I tend
to wake in panic   or from a dream   often the result is a number
   too much
          or too little
 of something   followed up by
                                    no follow up
left to wonder about   FREE T3

the 1 BLOOD CELL in my pee   the POTASSIUM in my blood

sometimes I'll get a call to retest which leads to
a 4am email
              it's a fatigue
                          greater than hypothyroid

* * *

THREE SHORTS :
missed the Ricard memorial because of couple's
therapy as well as the Guibert
                    opening   note —   free up
                                        Thursdays
                    *
          my dad used to say I had two
      speeds SLOW   and   STOP   so I moved
to my nemesis city   complain   complain   everyone get out
   your 5-yr plans   ::   mine is   moving rocks

                    *

nicest thing anyone has ever said to me
YOU DON'T HAVE CANCER YOU IDIOT

                    * * *

the structured walk
is also good for the human   it forces
                            shoulders out
    breasts implicated   more men
are saying "hi"   ask Mel and Nicole   do men ever just say hi?

stray dog   lottery

I win fear aggression   the dog is in me

                                        limits me

                                delimits me

walk by the high school

he perfectly at my side   partial basement cafeteria   plastic trays

                        pints of 2% milk

wouldn't be a parent

who let the kid cry   MAKE BED HOGS

                        when I wake at 4am   I'm clothed

                        with laptop dead   on thighs

neighbor women from Florida   raucous

on balcony connecting our bedrooms   one of these days I'm going

            to accept their invitation

                                to have frozen

                                berry drinks

                                on the roof

phobia as energy

that moves around

how to ask it move it out?   like the dog's various points of stress

                        putting on harness now fine   taking off harness not fine

but remember the dog is in me   music soothes

                                I forget about music

I make the grain free

porridge

                JP asked "do you feel better?" no

I feel
terrible!   and the table cracked up
              a little
              true   it's really thorny   to be mildly anything

out of therapy for
less than
              a month   taken over by
 heinous metaphors
              caution tape
              orange cones
                              "maybe   it's time"   for something new
had a long dream
was in a shirt with Buddha
on it and underwear   made many stops one of which
                      was to my former therapist   tricked me into using
the couch though she was
no analyst   then
disappeared   and reappeared   naked!

                      interesting things on our walk   a man
with yellow pocket
scissors   clipping off his filters   obese man absorbed in *The Edward Snowden Files*
                      dropping his beverage
              it rolling away
              guy on bench eating   noodles in a
                      green bowl out of his
                              bike basket   using the bag as a mitt

I pick up dog's shit

there's a hole in the bag   "I ♥ New York"   all the passers-by

for an entire block speaking

French

the porridge is meant as transitional

shouldn't be eaten too often   because it isn't meat

or veggie

or berry   I'm relishing in synchronicity

planning a reading of O'Hara's   *Lunch Poems*

everyone is happy with their poem assignment   naturally

even "Cornkind"

when he uses "moist" in the last line

is phenomenal   started day with a letter

from the person who gave me

Lunch Poems

decades ago   she said

when you're done

with it   just leave it

in a public bathroom

* * *

late F ate

the 20 extra minutes   jogged to Penn

Station to make

the train   DELAYED   do I have time

to buy almonds?

yes   a slow clerk
in a train station
    is an aggressive clerk

            30th Street Station has glorious wood
benches   half-assed planning of my reading   ended up blowing it
new reading glasses kept hitting mic

        horror of the soon-to-be published work feeling "dated"
an attempt to get where I am now?
were those simpler times?   no

Donna picks me up : "34th and Walnut again?"   meet latest dog   dinner in backyard
discover her partner and I were born   in the same hospital   we give
her a look   pick up their daughter's bow   shoot and miss 8 arrows
watch the kid
            get greater control   with less tension

the answer to my question is
"a giant Yew bush"   seized by this backyard   I think   I have what it takes
        to build a chicken coop   "you know electric?"   no   start tiny house
research   and tinier house   for the chickens
what about all of the books...

take picture of bridges over the Schuylkill   warm filter   used to live
here but not really   I stayed for her   all knowledge was of her
              not the city

                        is it summer yet ?   not accordingly

                        *   *   *

mess of broken watches
find my fix it ticket   the preschoolers grip the rope and walk
around and around   my block singing   something
about bees   bits of dried leaves in change bowl
you'll know when your probiotic has at least 6
strains   have fit when solar calculator stops working at dusk
and the budget keeps on ticking   music as
realignment strategy   listening to a band
an ex-lover I haven't seen in decades is going to see
in London   with a new lover   who is also a Cancer
with tattoos   my heart burns with pleasure
the only miracle I've witnessed this spring are the squash
plants blanketing the balcony   straw slippers
from a typical metropolis   last grainy sip   I've done it
again   one year in every two   I am unprepared to teach

head uptown then down   what was he like   well he
moves sloth-like   and bows his head to listen
my new therapist   a new round   of hide and seek
reference Winnicott   I'm ready to be found   from now on

I'm time- stamping everything I write   sorry fern   sorry
shrub rose   I'll remember to bring a pot of water
in here when I'm boiling chicken   an unforeseen
con of white shoes is spilling coffee on them   when
the treasurer handed me two "nervous
pills"   before the meeting   I felt grateful
for the direction   my life has taken
the dog prefers her in the night   when I wake
he is in a ball at the bend   in her knee
I touch him lightly   working so hard on reversing
the effects of being kicked   so he can open to a range
of nonthreatening energies   tiny house strategies   put shrub
rose on balcony   in time the sky opens
for a shot   at life   therapist says something about
becoming the animal that eats us   oh!
I'll become a PANTHER   this therapy
a major expense   "you can't
afford not to"   scanning for needless
expenditures   no more juice bar   hello
library card   nothing wrong with jeans
and the same blue button down every day   already
ditched drinking   the movies   vacations   new Fuji maybe
we'll meet some day   hello   are you my
mystical experience?

Jozef Van Wissem and Jim Jarmusch song
circling my sweet spot   watch the preschoolers
romp   collate Alice Leslie and Philip with Dogen

Basho Shiki   you'll just make it GO
on the plane   unidentified caller was B
wants to make sure I found someone   intrusive!
well people   can see I'm a mess   it's familiar
the ceiling gets in your hair   the congregation hates you
you wave the Polaroid and nothing develops

K dreams I win something   not since that
blue ribbon for the softball throw...   in the humidity
I smelled the linen   yesterday in the Copy Cottage
a young woman with at least 20 tattoos took
care of me   "strength to the meek"
and a heart with "success" in it   browning ground
beef at the stove   K says she feels
I'll have easy travels   guy in baseball
uniform   "Whackers"   nurse in blue
scrubs and pink hoodie   a few squirrels and birds
seen on our walk   it's Father's Day   has this dog
sired any pups?   how can I   of all people
explain anything   he plows his snout into
my forearms my hands   when I try to read
a peaceful gesture   my body is pissed
because it took so long to   discover
it had special knowledge   sharpen the no. 2   to a nub
was that a floater   or   a dust bunny?   you think
spring is over but it's   just a feeling
until the sun   can go no further North

SUMMER

Frisbee barefoot on the grassy
    knoll   woman sunning with shirt over
head   a fun game goes to shit
                         my throw is ten feet to the right
of Renee   see what happens
        when you think about it
            it's a student over there   I hope
I've behaved
          some nerve   taking people on a walking
meditation   like some Zen Practitioner   FOLLOW ME TO THE CREEK
      knew the way   at least   the statement standing in for what I don't know

far more shameful   oh kid your line today made me want
                to adopt you if you need a whatever I am…
"best for last best for last"   ah son   I get the message

didn't cross my mind
youth would feel
limited by lineage   conflation with blood   we say the present has its own
identity   we   in perpetual discovery

go long DIVE she said   been a bitch for 2 years   what?! yes   accept the gist

 SHOW don't TELL   as life precept
              indeed   flawed   still argue for it   what's good for the poem has
       to have some value
            interpersonally   question mark   silence

* * *

            where are you spider spider?
foot in web
it nightly builds in tub   we finally meet   you should build this over there

have to run hair dryer to
get light   don't report   I'm an adapter   the New York
headache now termed   the Boulder head-
ache   dehydration from good cries   impact of intense appreciation

though let this be

my feedback form

I LOATHE THE COLLOQUIUM

I do and will try to   stay connected   maybe I'll know someone
for 50 years
some
day   : Jen closes her eyes while editing Renee mumbles to herself writing up another
calamity me at the end of a brown ink pen on over sized graph paper and a pot of pu-erh
tea the most ancient cup group of senior men laughing bookstore person asking
        "Do you know afternoon Tom not morning Tom?"
sharing nuts look to R "oh you're showing me your anxiety" in the form of a blood clot
will it kill me?

"if you have to claim it call it your not-clot"   Matvei so into my Kotaro book consider
giving it to him   still feel his mouth mouthing words against my cheek
last night   "fucking genius"
New York can be so cordoned   lets have wine   in July
writing in this graph paper notebook because of you man   killing this pen   3:30am?
ya I was up not nobly to write but thinking I smelled something burning   women keep
walking off with Hoa   the tarot   me? no way   everyone has an afternoon
plan   together in psyche   mere moments by the creek and I have to return
to the hotel to pee   try to halt the mind's knowledge of   a flood
of emails   days ago   was another time

* * *

finally I love
Glenn Branca   hip to his tuning system   cook to it
pour two glasses   eat the Shakshuka   heat   drifts me
forget it on simmer
        but you cannot destroy
the yolk of an egg
        within the vibration of a string
is the entire harmonic series
dog barked at a running boy
again   responsibility bar raised   the walk has to
have style   I bark   at the same person too
such is an anger
        received so
                young

       guitars thrashing   peaceful in
equilibrium
       black sabbatical
          you can never stop working

* * *

reading a long book about real life
catastrophe   maybe
it'll stop me from dreaming
up my own   hot afternoon   drift
wake   DRINK WATER FOOL the problem
with doing things you love all day
is like being   on speed
worrying can make you think you're exerting
some control   over the situation   like not enjoying yourself can make time
drag   perverse fountain of youth   when there was no joy
and a whole life ahead   drift
then an ice cream spoon
               falls to the floor

* * *

it's all coming together   the catastrophe book   waiting
              for Alexis   she said   rain or shine
brought an umbrella though

it was clear   it was not
when I arrived   to the gardens   Alexis
          the type to research   the weather   voice mail from
mother   why didn't I respond   to her text about grandma's chafing
                    within the average time   90 seconds
so I'm photographing myself as this thing

                              slow brews   glass covered   breeze-
                                        way   back-
                                        drop
Storm Arthur down south   to the west   storm that downed my parents
                              electric   storm I'm reading
about   and the one in the dream
when I found safety on a
                    cement embankment of a reservoir   drops
commence   Alexis arrives
it's member night   when it starts coming down
          catch up in chilled sub-gallery   missed call from K   phone lit
with NYC.gov flash flood alerts   lightening struck
One World Trade   her and dog afraid
                    splitting half a too salty bird   wet white
                    suede shoes with holes   the thing about marriage
is I can no longer simmer into
                              jackass stew   the thing
about analysis
is you have to smoke out the truth   squish   squish
I hear you coming

the thing I didn't want to face   is   YOU WILL BE DISAPPOINTING
     that's all
          they grind the coffee this late
                              man behind me   "too late to drink"
give me a bag   of your darkest   my deadline got bumped
tomorrow morning I'll get to be a writer
                                        in the grand style

* * *

with a thwack   I remember the funny bone
the largest unprotected nerve in the human body
          holy   fucking   shit
                              it's the 4th   of July
butcher is closed so pick up some subpar thighs   how to get at
my ambivalence   it was like Sicilian-American Christmas
                    by Lake Michigan
texted alert that due to high
                    rip current
fireworks will move south of Brooklyn
                    Bridge   balcony a choice view
          far into my own
implosive sorrow   see the dog is scared   tend to the dog
                closing us in
                the middle room
coaxed out by K's excitement   but just for a few minutes
                we can't have him

54

developing another phobia

                                      let's watch

                      a comedy   after contemplating

Siberian prison escape   pick *Barefoot in the Park*   keep giving Jane Fonda

            a chance   can't get to the end   the barefoot part

with her as guide   earnestness is always a cover   try *Julia*

              same earnestness   Fonda as Hellman trying to be a good writer

smoking   drinking   temper tantrums   friend Julia

a memoir invented from whole cloth?   fighting Nazis   Hellman unrepentant

                          Stalinist?!?   HELL she did sue

                     Mary McCarthy for saying she was

over-rated   on public television

           The Group is not streaming   my companions now both sleeping

                last time I watched it   I paused on the scenes of St. Mark's

                looking so quaint

                               *   *   *

the map says catch the D from Dekalb

sign says B   MTA worker tells me no I have to take the Q

wait for the Q   and the D comes   was she right or wrong

I get on the D   she was wrong   triumphant on Prince!

picking up a cord   maybe some shorts for the lake

shopping in Soho is wicked   feel the judgment run both ways

all the shorts are ugly   find some pants   uniform fetish vibe

I know what I'd do with money   cultivate an excessive

wardrobe   guy on F home asks if anyone is listening is anyone
awake   for his speech about illegal incarceration   hold eye contact
tail end of independence day weekend   kid glares at him   his girl-
friend leaning into his shoulder   all of our fantasies
offered counterpoint   look for reasons not to feel
anxious   nature's remedy   is people   pull handle in case of
emergency   I've worked hard   on my infrastructures   and it's hard
so don't pull that handle   pull out green notebook   Hank
said he's sitting on a donut "like a dickweed"   glad I jotted
that down   and "follow up with Hank"   "do you want to be
a thing that limps   or do you want to be a player?" said Claudia
another Sicilian   and "you're Sicilian you shouldn't even have to work"
and god I ROARED that afternoon in the empty bar : "all I want
is a little reaction" Tina Turner in Rite-Aid   man on F last week
chatting up young woman   "41 years in NYC and I've never seen the Statue
of Liberty" and "New Jersey? No offense but you look like a California
woman"   I've been quoting Cher in *Moonstruck* since 1987
except I slap myself in the face   SNAP OUT OF IT   her way
of saying BE PRESENT   my proto-Buddha   just accept that I'm not
going to like you   for what boils down to   in geologic time
another 45 minutes

* * *

butterflies Monday through Friday
morning in my stomach
        is it the conditions of life   before I check my work email

or my relationship with

my org   called a building a facility today

talking to a friend   and a room within   a venue

REPORTS

GALORE

and chores   fill bucket with hot water

                     one foot in tub

             one out   slip but catch balance

no rags   use old pair of cotton underwear   my life in dog hair

          get to kitchen table   knock over chair

              balanced there   hits back of

                  my head

I guess I'd rather be

doing something else   like nothing

* * *

take my seat across from therapist   no flowers in the vase

this week   I once wanted to say "nice peonies" to him

but refrained   I had some dreams   he produces

a notebook   "I like to write them down"   this is beyond

a joy   this other person writing down my dreams   K will

say that is so typical   of my exhibitionism   but I say

maybe like my socialism too   lets all take notes

on the dreams of others   as they speak them   open the royal

road and the rural route   so I go to some kind of claims

desk and say I'm here for my dog Isabel   other people

are getting their dogs back   taxidermied   wrapped
in plastic   I say NO   my dog is alive   there has been some
terrible city-wide event   "can you see any faces?"   gosh I like
his questions   yes like a Pekingese face with under bite   bulging
eyes   I don't like that breed so much   favored by Chinese Buddhist
Monks   they return with Isabel on a leash and she
looks so great   is so happy to see me   she's so vital and I
have recovered her   without question she is mine
and I was   right   she is alive   "it's unexpected" he says
yes that is not the usual outcome   his notebook is
from a drugstore   a good choice   it communicates that nothing
is more important than what is written within   whereas my
notebook that holds this dream   is 11½ x 13   graph paper
he writes down another of my dreams   I know he's a dog-
lover   we spend most of the session talking   about dogs

* * *

my herbalist friend and I revel in the heat   "it's so good for your
constitution"   she buys me early birthday lunch   I've known her
for some time   got to get home to my furry friend   I worry
he's howling   I'm just like someone I used to make fun of
who refused to use postcards because the post office   lost one   once
she was old   now I'm old   don't tell me I'm not   I'm old
enough where I see the ugly tendencies   that want to take over my personality
"she never used to be like that"   it's what I think

about the women in my family   who couldn't see to take care of
their minds   taking care of others   devastation of the   either/or
saw a woman in midtown holding herself   up   nothing
innately sad about it   but the conditions   moving slow
and with great effort   in a consumer market   I'm looking
for the 5   ask a guy in a driver's uniform   where's the entrance?
how-can-you-be-so-dumb tone   "it's those doors   Grand Central Station"
I thought you went in there to get out of town   but I got to lunch
in Brooklyn with my friend   who I've known for some time

* * *

our own private Amityville
   of flying ants
         we   opening our eyes   they swarming
out of a crack by the bed
      no bode well for abode   nothing that citrus and tape
won't cure   leave note for the dog sitter   sorry you have to
deal   another what if   4L used poison   driving them to
their "gay neighbors"   what if   going to hometown feels death-
      defying and so does staying put   I can ruin
   any fun time just ask   it's nice to share a suitcase
K hates to fly   we won't crash   be worried about
driving with my dad   right   that is not
        a comfort   what if
I could draw a system   of belief   that has no redemption
upper echelons bearing prophets of perdition

that would be   my family tree   big hug for grandma
          your skin looks…   "oh I know
    my neighbor complemented my skin
and the next
day I had eczema"   …looks *good*   who is it that doles out
the eczema   and the envy?   trees planted in the 70s
add a lushness   you wouldn't have seen all these houses
in disrepair   the door is open and the staircase carpet is the same
    this was the repo man's house   said twice
                my mom never one to forget the slights of
neighbors   me clipping John Lennon assassination articles   but
not for Reagan the following year   or for the Pope   the joke the bad
          boys started   "now he's more holy"
this is a boring tour   other than how the words "Mysteries of Small
          Houses" now howl through me   the perpetual turning the corner
in the airport by shelves of foam core cheese hats   don't sing to me!
I would like to be celebrated
          in spoken words   song is camouflage
I shot the squirrel   I did   to make it as a Midwestern boy
  don't remember the supper club   Wild Rose is close
                to Upper Mill Pond   on floating chair
                    with a Bloody Mary   5 senior female mutts
      work it out   don't want to hear the story about the eagle
and the puppy   again   getting a signal on the mound
    what if   my dog   needs me   what perversity
to come on this rupture-of-spleen   anniversary   the what if is all
    about this   I looked out for death   and it dusted my mind

with cool powder   fly back to second home
            quick fever   an only symptom   can I
touch my chin to my chest   yes!   not spinal meningitis   what if
            took me two hours to cauterize myself
      wet towel and flannel shirt   BEEP BEEP BEEP
it's normal   new guy who lives in basement with the
Brussels Griffon sees me eyeballing his tee-shirt with Divine on it   saw myself
      seeing him   gleaner on the street says   "give him some water…
            and give yourself some too"

* * *

   didn't know Ducati
         till I read Andrew's poem
now there's a new red
         Ducati Monster
      always outside our building

* * *

noted   woman in tunic   and floppy hat   on phone
an over-correction   hit the F   so not 15 late   to Bluebird

      it's Brenda!   I'm in here   and I have finished
   a cortado

too crowded   go to another place with antisocial design   take the corner
of the bar   talk loud about trouble   and ideas for

investigative
          poems   but I don't want to have to use a PO box for life   the cocaine

          seizure
                    story   seems innocuous   but consider Olson's

          The Special View of History   and

today's sickening news   it started long ago
and went unrecognized   as a process :   Palestinians of Gaza

          10:24pm   :   296 dead
                          2,230 wounded

flight MH17 shot down   over eastern Ukraine   wiping out 108
of the world's   AIDS researchers   and   activists

          story in a unit of place in time   giant hole
          in Siberia has scientists scratching their   heads

a life has a scale   a function is how a thing acts   NYPD
put asthmatic man   in a chokehold   Thursday

thought to have been selling "loosies" untaxed cigarettes   civilian video

of police murdering another black man   viral   July 17, 2014

"There are things that people will not accept

and will not believe unless they see an image of it."   Levi in the Rail 2

                                                                        days ago

                    what Emmett Till's mother knew

            Brenda points out an old Star of David   above the luggage store

                    where you can bargain if you have cash

"here's the pickle guy"   the surfer coffee shop is disorganized

today   hit corner store for almonds   my arm bumps against

            another woman's arm   "EXCUSE YOU"   I wasn't paying attention

                "I'm sorry"   but a smile is trailing because Brenda is

amused that I need almonds   so it doesn't come off as

                                                                sincere as it is

                                    *   *   *

a few hours into sugar detox   amend to 20g a day

spit out bite of green apple   struggles in the neighborhood today   woman staggers

down Smith   usual guy on the street agitated   sunset   new guy on high school

steps   "wanna buy some incense   I'm a war vet"   what can I expect

I fight to become more civil   in the decline   goo
bubbling up in Gowanus toilets   before minds merge with computers
I'll have been the best lover of life   check herb box   the oregano   grows
apparently neither of the women who live here watered such regal squash in time
replant and water   vestiges   soil sticks to leg hair stubble   shaved on a whim
see the dog suffer remorse and rehab in a flash   for guarding his butcher
bone   drops it and crawls to me submissive   my position forgives him
they should have left the two bleached American
flags flying over the Brooklyn Bridge   the most surveilled site in the land
was accessed   "Police Seek Teen Skateboarder"   July 25, 2014   those big tin pans
for cooking turkeys   were used to cover the spotlights

* * *

stare at leaning tower
        of books   an aid to disassociation
during same old fight
        who ruined whose day

        Diderot's *The Nun*
        Perec's *La Boutique Obscure*
        Baldwin's *Another Country*
        the little Hanuman books on top

* * *

cut in the East Village today
         before my stylist   goes on maternity leave   take it short
obsesses on "sideburns"   no time for style   strutting my stuff downtown
                           with clean flat hair

check on office   Jimmy painted over
the sockets   but damn   when can I move in?

      PO on Broadway reeks of pot   mail in proof that we did it
and we gave proper credit   see everyone wants credit   where it's due
punk on St. Mark's   "what the fuck it's only a buck"
we seem to reward
         the homeless   for ingenuity everyone has "an ask"
                 punk with white pit
                 in a floral dress   bag of kibble open by
     her head   dead?   can't even...

so yeah   there is stevia in this drink   and it's already in me

guy picking scabs all over hands   swing into the Met
come out with imitation crab meat salad
which I gobble on foot   wait   what the hell is this!?

FEAR OF SOY   it's cheap molded whitefish with loads
of sodium   strike!   gulp fizzy water
         spills from the corners of my mouth
               onto my chest

* * *

"Boo   listen
next time
you walk me"   an older butch says to me   I get
how she's seeing me   but ya   I'd do that for her

* * *

never have drank too much   or smoked at all   but I do this thing
where I drink black coffee with my replacement
                                                    thyroid hormone
did my own reading on this and learned   it blocks absorption
habit is habit   did my own reading and learned
it's an autoimmune disease   my body attacks my
                    butterfly shaped gland   and will till the end
of time   like an autoimmune disease
K makes coffee most mornings   before she goes to work
    we drink it together   sometimes we don't talk
                                    then I take my pill

＊　＊　＊

it's hard to get to know someone
  to the point of prediction should've known she wouldn't like
the movie where the woman uses 100%
    of her brain and turns into a flash drive
too many special effects equivalent to me speaking loudly too close
to her face poets worth their salt
  know that we exist because of time but Luc Besson isn't
 a poet today I bought gold sneakers online on credit too expensive
it's not that I don't have the cash for payment it's just as bad
the cash is retirement cash I began to be able to imagine
   a personal future which involved heightened awareness of
citizenship in the world is quality of life
   is wishful thinking a celebrity who plays
  a lesbian on TV how did you do your research? snicker snicker
well I've had a checkered past well-told tale of drug rehab and apparently
  lesbianism my dad consoled my mom by saying at least she's not
an addict when did you know you were a criminal? it was before
the surveillance before being on lists you can
  never get off I am safely paranoid
HELLO MR. LANDLORD remember when
storm waters were rushing down the stairwell
  you asked me to go to the roof and unclog the one drainpipe
me in my boxers with a broom up to my knees in water
   plunging out dead leaves
artist lawyer journalist educator propagandize
  or be criminal "that's a whole lot of shake

shake   shake…" man to women   "when you go in there
          don't talk to any guys"   a mother instructs her young
                    daughter and MR. LANDLORD months later when I locked myself
out and you charged me $75   to let me back in
                    that was a revelation   not the kind
of landlord I was   you can ask Mike Hauser
I began to be able to imagine
          a personal future   with heightened empathy
amidst predictions that media studies will replace English
departments   reading strengthens the
          attention span   makes us harder to
control   makes us more empathetic   the chokehold has been illegal for 20 years
yet the NYPD used it again   on a pregnant woman   a black woman grilling
outside her home   what is "grilling?"   grilling like cooking
          it too was caught on video   for the public to see

* * *

preschool walks lines of 15 kids holding a rope
  day in   day out
          what I know now
July is over   no wind in sail…   a ton of bricks…
clanging platitudes   the good fortune of this canteen
                    in my canvas pack   tap tap tap
water for people   try to contain
                    multitudes
                    of projections

＊ ＊ ＊

forget half of what I write as I write
in my head walking   if I wrote on my hand
I'D FORGET
MY HAND
                    layered bling for gym
couple having date on rowing   machine
        "Pelosi can shut it"   defending the party
unplug my buds   the butcher has frozen   "PYTHON"
        steaks   "this little light of mine"   trying to recall
if the man asking for change outside the Met market
who makes me uneasy   has a beard   in case I ever have to
describe him   "God made you beautiful"   "get out of my world
                                            you don't know it"
dream of Eileen twice   she did it
                            so will I   no skin   to thin
        skin   one week back and I've already
    have to call legal
and psych
            "you should let it shine"   best part of my world
        waking at 6am to read a biography   LOOK AT THIS LIFE   quite a life
been meaning to meditate for 2 years   should one know
                    what I know   "on the level everyday"

huddled on rush hour F with pocket
    communism   sometimes when a man's backpack protrudes
                into your gut   you have to be the big spoon

* * *

"Tony Blair should... should..."
        grandfatherly Irish Senator cries out
            "keep his face out of the Middle East!"

retweet   venture a first hashtag
some consolation had been
       thinking that   all times seemed like the worst
of times for the people living through them   my 90+ year old grandmas say
NO   this is
the   worst   time   they don't   understand   why
they are   still   every   night   they   tell god
they   are
               every night I have to figure out what
      to eat for dinner   waiting for the dry cleaning
baseball game on mute   iconic images of repetitive motions
       those with   good arms
why the Met didn't have green olives   it's turning   into luxury apartments
leaving the neighborhood
            w/ bodegas and gourmet
caught my reflection in plate glass
            think Kurt in his travel clothes
being chased into the
mountains by Nazis

it's raining and I'm carrying a box
with a dog bed which I keep dropping
"why are you looking at me with that
ugly face?"   my face has absorbed the run off   an algal bloom

bedroom outlet smokes
because I know the best way to stop or contain
electrical fire is to cut the power
I have stopped fire 3 times   we stay
rent is okay for here   and the vet is blocks away
trade is   layman electricity
key opens 2 other apartment doors   the intercoms
don't work   landlord replaces the outlet   and leaves
what about our…!!!!!   he's OUT   *why does…*
you should be plugging it into this one
this keep…   ma'am trip the breakers   how many BTUs   wait
now I'm his apprentice   *keep…*   can I get you some water
money is real tight   *happening…?*   that tape is to keep
the flying ants…   just use this one

the bra you put on at 8am by 8pm has you
in vice grip   think I see a star from a crime drama
can't think of name   everyone's coming up Scully
and Mulder   sleeping
with the balcony door open afraid
to plug in the air   afraid that even on the 4th floor an intruder…
at midnight it shows   a giant cicada
singing its song

69

a hollow abdomen what a relief   for the anxiety of keeping
            everyone   safe   wrap   a   sardine
in a paper towel   go
        looking   for the stray

* * *

Tree of Heaven has grown to provide   visual
barrier   between me and backyard neighbors
7:30 particularly quiet
Tuesday morning gust unfurls ratty American
flag in park also the black one
beneath it   POW/MIA   equally ratty
wearing Leslie's robe that T gave me   sitting
unladylike   the plants   even   the   oregano
need more attention   can't blame the heart
or the heat   temperate summer   can't get in touch
with the constituency   probably floating in lakes
and oceans across the land   looks peaceful in here
but we're reprogramming three brains   DO NO MORE
HARM   we see   how events inspire inner fascisms
            paired with power
viola   carry a white flag get shot   throw your hands up and
still get shot   in this microcosm   we apologize even
when we don't understand why the other   is hurt by us

* * *

young women walking kids
      15 hands on a rope
          singing about bees   struggling with the 3 year
         budget   thinking about years
in threes   a stretch   onus to describe great
futures   on me   I had 48 hours
on   Fire Island   "this is not exactly what we talked about"
        Claudia says   "baby st ps"
an old timey airplane with a banner
      advertising tequila   me in my shades

* * *

         didn't know you could get such bad
        Italian food in NYC   visiting cousin says "you need to call
your grandma   try mornings or you'll get her
      sundowning"   10am eastern time she
       has anxiety attack 3 minutes in   "do you want my
dad to come over?" but he's racing
at Road America   maybe at 70
     I'll be doing something
        my loved ones find insane   maybe my eyes
will be computerized   and I'll never
be too tired to read all night   I call her back
 there are things she remembers

about a family once so big
no one needed friends

* * *

see a Philip Seymour Hoffman movie   maybe his last   he walks out of the frame
        after shattering disappointment   he trusted the American
all you need to know is that our bombs and our aid packs are the same yellow
            "once your belief in humanity vanishes / all time
        becomes borrowed..."   I reread a Jennifer Moxley poem
5 years older than me   her work a deep comfort
having to do with one's body knowing   the 70's   the phase
    when   a nation's disgust   with its government was high
how did Reagan do it?   wipe away our depth
  one's body knowing   its middle   getting up to pee each night
in the pet store   an old woman
        holds up the line with questions
  about cat food   hands me a postcard about the climate
        march   I shrink
from demonstrations   maybe a flaw
            in my world view   where the more an evil is repeated
the more unstoppable
        inbox is full of news of interest to poets
  copied on emails about a poet's
        health   "removed the packing"   I tell everyone in the office
he's going to die soon   what will we do
                without him?

* * *

elbow radiates heat against
             the left side of my face   it's too close   bad subway
protocol   when I get off on 2nd
             I look at the face   who could be so oblivious
                    a teen   grocery store
         shuttered   have to remember to pick up
basics in the East Village
             Anne calls   usually asks 2 questions
are you taking your fish oil   and   how is your marriage
   well — 3
how is the Project

* * *

8:45am   I can do this for 15
                    more minutes and then
I log in   have 2 messy issues
             to contend with today
both involving people
             of unbalanced mind
to be kind   I'm trying to
         find   what motivates them
know the delusion
                    to join the delusion

* * *

one month since Michael Brown murder   aspect of
                                                                    ongoing apocalypse

police stalk   detain incarcerate   kill
people of color   profitable business of
                                        holding humans captive

teaching the
remainder to hold themselves
captive   since I left the note
                    "I will not complain"   on my desk
          I find myself sitting at the kitchen table

retreat into pots of coffee   pencils   notebooks
my grandma didn't cry
                              last time we spoke
          open your windows I said
knock on the door   I bet that's Gladys
they'll play a word game
and order pizza   "I have no one"   you have
Gladys   sister-in-law for 70 years   no   one   open the door!
no   one
just said goodbye to last of her 8 siblings
messed up by war   he moved away
          alcoholic   to Colorado

                    maybe it's longevity that gives me
anxiety   what if I live 50 more years   no country
for old dykes

        news story about a man who proposed to a woman
while mountain climbing   they ended up in trouble
the woman hurt   they thought they were going to die
        the story is about   the adventurous
method of engagement   the newscaster
admonishes them   for not setting a date
                        now that they are safe

                    *   *   *

garbage men came last night
this morning dark stains   on the cement   walk by the language
center   beginning Italian   well   I haven't tried
in my 40's   one small yellow   wild
                        rose   on the shrub
    article that creative people
        stay up late   just as I've mastered the 10pm to 6am
today I woke at 5:15   and enjoyed the dark   did some dishes
    just as the sun rose at 6:30 I walked the dog
                deposited a check   back here K
in the shower and coffee grounds soaking   in the French press
    read that full moon in Pisces may explain yesterday's
foul moods

                    I set out   another notebook

       where I write things to do for work

before I left for the walk   Nicole asked me if there is ever a time

when she'll feel that she has gotten everything done   I say no

       and think of my favorite myth   the guy who is punished

and has to repeat his task forever

does the realization of the absurd require suicide? Camus answers "No. It requires

revolt."

        what a weird predicament

          last night after I turned the lights off

I counted invisible sheep   I tried to remember a certain day in my life

                 the day   I moved from Milwaukee

to Philadelphia   reduced to one detail   throwing sturdy plastic garbage

      bags full of books into the trunk   of my light blue Oldsmobile

did I say goodbye to my parents

      what did I tell the woman

        I was dating   who I gave my apartment to   did I have good-

bye drinks with friends?   who were my friends?   a friend drove with me

it was Emily   did we stop to eat   sleep   what did we talk about

the day I left my life

                 * * *

cause   dept. of sanitation truck   a cacophony of horns

          YOU SIR   ARE AN ASSHOLE!

    on phone cancelling

double billed dinner order from last night when
my two large meatballs and chop salad arrive
                    in record time
                         Magda Olivero has died
I put on "Alfano"   the dog charges into the bedroom
    last week my therapist   cancelled after a 6 week hiatus
because he had a fever   so specific   a fever   today after I spoke
about my future plans   he said   "your tenses
        double down on provisionality
        it's redundant"

                              *   *   *

F going express from Bergen to Broadway/
Lafayette   little more legwork   Swatch store
a magnet   try on two at a time   guy says "you should get
both   you know   Swatch
stands for   second watch"
I did not know   I get black hands on black face
go ahead   ask me what time it is!
maybe I'll come back for the one
where part of my money will go toward clean water   it's food
pantry day   at the church   people line up their carts to hold their spots
never see any of the regulars   who hang around
the church   in line   this is for those who need *more* food
who have a place to steam a cart of   yellowing greens   the
guy I see on the street everyday tells me   he likes my hat   men

seem to like this hat   it's a man's hat
and I'm a man's man   I've been alerted that
the front gate will   be kept locked even though the work
on the portico is complete   keeps the riff-raff out
I'm a riff's raff   a poet's poet   and my feet are trained to
go in the front   a ladies man   a layman   and a lady man
and my feet are trained to go   in the front

therapist refers to my "hell realm"   the thing about naming it
now I can say   "I want out" and now I got the claws   the phone rings
it's someone calling   "hi is this Stacy?
                              you've made a really bad mistake"
"you've caused irreparable damage   to the organization"
I make the sound of milk steaming   my hand slowly moving
the imaginary pitcher   if I was a barista   what if
I couldn't make foam shapes   what is the collateral
damage   of escape
on the day of this writing   I can't
answer   dream my ex-lover   the one I saw
on Thursdays for 2 years   and I   were in a canoe filling
with water   she dreams we're just hanging
out   I make her laugh in her dreams   I'm trying to use my body
as a bucket   it's Friday night and I'm sitting on the floor
                                        at the brink of fall

I have overslept and missed the sunrise at 6:36   roasted
vegetables at 9pm to eat with eggs this morning   opened door

and closed   chilly   mourn the end of the season

no amount of cinnamon   peppers   hot sauce   wool   blubber   can

make me warm in winter   inner thermostat has an old plastic dial

gear up   stock the freezer with meats   budget how many sweaters

I can afford   dog claws at the tree

where the squirrel   shakes down the nuts

between parallel and merged lives

there must be good company

winter is coming   torpor   denning

try to share   shed

lone wolf

who knew it would be so challenging to live

simply   to live as you want

one of my teachers in college announced "no one

in this room will be writing poetry in 10 years"

* * *

my superego is so severe   I had to externalize it

along with a weak chin   too fat for most

of my salad days   gym has mirrored walls   it's not narcissism

it's surveillance   police are what they

are because   like presidents   structure takes the man

could smell this morning's rain last night   dozed

off watching a serial crime

drama   walked the dog   eyeballed walls for mosquitos

back   to bed   grateful for no dreams   after finding out

I knew the "woman found dead"　　once we played badminton
on a beach　　"can the Project host a memorial"　memorials
　　　　so difficult　　because we don't process
absence　　administrating isn't processing
　　　　the word "near" in "near her home"　haunting
swathe tragedy like a martyr
2 eyeballs doing a 180　　taking theoretical position of　one
about to die　　rendering tragedy impossible　　I need a job
　　　　　I don't do as well
just registered for Italian
　　　　after searching "can old people learn a second language"
therapist says maybe my books are　my method
　　　　　of travel　　well that's unacceptable
don't try to make me feel better　　many radios playing in 4-story
　　　walk-up with smells of toast　I think
　　　　　　　　　　la dolce vita!　　saxophonist
　　　　　　　　　　mimics train door closing　　I think
　　　　　　　　　　la dolce vita
　　a human life like high speed films of　plants　　la dolce vita
café near NYU　　sipping iced mint tea early for a meeting across the street
　　　　　table of 7 young people with pens
　　and notebooks　　projection is　they're planning something revolutionary
　　　　the café has magazines　　for us to read but we are to only
take one at a time　　we are being watched　　layers of redundancy
therapist prefers we speak of superego in German
for precision　*Über-Ich*
　　　　the Over-I　　standing atop the id　　it's good
to be able to stop eating

cake   to not punch someone in the face   last week I pulled out one
of my books   *Scene of the Crime*
unopened since I moved to this city
        where I stuck a clipping from *The New York Times Magazine*   September 13 1998
"Unabomber's cabin now sits in warehouse limbo…"
        I didn't remember that I had any knowledge of his cabin
when I wrote of it earlier this spring

                              * * *

Friday night   :

                this is ourselves
                under pressure

there are readings occurring within walking distance   listening to isolated vocal tracks
of Bowie and Mercury   upset that I needed to participate in an old trick
they who disguise nefarious plots   presto!   as things that everyone craves

there is a line I keep in the margin waiting to use
                "my dog has a Roman nose"
                        I think a nod to Whalen
                                something about a lion's Roman nose

I have till Monday night   alone in a room where I share a makeshift desk
till the fall
equinox   equal night   recent peace   getting up in the dark

Saturday night   :

out with friends   2 Manhattans

my day mood smoothed over
best not to read articles about how to engage narcissists
on the weekend   and hackles were up after K moved some books from my Susan Howe
        and Etel Adnan stacks   even though I said sure no big deal
I retreated into my knowledge   of the stacks   my voluminous
        relationships

                when engaging narcissists try to limit your words to "yes"
and "no"   don't do what I do
don't try to show them   a way out   of their vortex
        don't think that everyone wants   to be a better person

* * *

ears perk up on Sunday call with mom   each time
                she says   "MOTHER HOUSE"
                        "you know   where they
                put nuns out to pasture"

        just went to her 50th
                high school reunion   we cluck like hens

but as my heart beats

                      there's no escape from abusive clergy

                  Alexis said last night

                       colonial power sleeps in the tyranny of paperwork

after seeing Laurie Anderson with Kronos Quartet   drink at Frank's

        Laurie   she's very nice

pitfalls

       my thinking takes   dividing idols into nice

                          / mean

Jim Carroll was very nice as was Robert Ashley

Philip Glass is very nice   and it's nice when I see him dining on 2nd

or buying flowers

             in a split moment

               we give   a yes or a no   to a whole

                        person

       Anderson's style   impresses something upon me   about aging

         gracefully   which has something to do with style   all in black and

using a voice filter / "audio drag"   speaks of voluminous extinctions

I don't understand what the conditions are

for art   to change me   but I feel so much better this morning

FALL

wind parts long beard in two
passing on the avenue

* * *

"you made 64 meatballs?"

every person

at a party

is entitled

to 3 meatballs   and if you can't eat 3 at least
you know they were
there for you   excess is something   about my mother

when I experience
the part of the self
that is temporal   the part
that isn't   stares at a hairbrush

I'll be hit with it
or my long brown hair will be brushed   waiting for the moment the adults

falter and the children rise up   ///   she says to me

on the phone but speaking of me in the third

person   "I wondered why my baby was asking me
about menopause?   oh   my   baby
is   45"

MAMA WILL THE HOT FLASHES BE BAD

I took out my daily planner
            during a meeting   everyone else was using their devices
I'm used to it being noticed   perhaps because in an art gallery   I felt self-
conscious   perhaps   to establish   common ground

we laughed about the obscurity
            of the land line   when you'd call your best friend and her dad would
answer   "Is Jenny home?"
                        ///   she says

"I'd have to check my calendar from that year"   the last time she saw
                                                so and so

        explains that it's good to write things down   walking the dog in the rain
this morning   he's not averse   and with rubber boots   nor am I
        the phrase   "happy place"   is so annoying

                        but if you can get over that
                        TO the place…
        the barn   it's not clear what

my work is there   but my body   in this place
      is always moving
           in pleasing ways

* * *

reading a novel that
should be a quick read   dog-
         eared   pages   un-dog-ear
   themselves   between sessions   which only occur on the train

when I'm not watching people   or not refining my to-do
        list   I did read a slender volume   in a day

the author says she went to the St. Marks John Cage birthday
reading   if I hadn't been alone this would've activated my speech
      about ORGANIZATIONAL SENSITIVITY

because   DANSPACE   people made that event happen   did anyone
    else's dentist have the sign
    ignore your teeth and they'll go away   the landmark

isn't going anywhere   nor is the landlord   although Fran Lebowitz
      the one time we talked   thought this naïve
    I said but what about   the remains of all the politicians
and she said   builders would dig them up   she asked if I smoked
   right there

in the yard   I said no never
she asked me if I wanted her to teach me
and I said no   which today   I regard   as a career mistake

                she had just come off stage
where her last quip   everyone was aflutter
    was about living alone
        that being a remarkable thing for a lesbian

* * *

dahlias are wilted   interspersed mint holding up   just cold enough
to get me thinking of winter

a budget is
        confronting the truth
                of your weekly expendable
I'll eat less meat   rather than
            stop buying books with abandon
    I'll cut off
        the fingers   of the gloves my brother gave me
in New York you want
    your digits unencumbered   only drink the well whiskey

during happy hour at 12th Street $2.50   or $3.50 on the rocks
    as the bartender explained
        a larger pour   therapy is like a second rent

when will I be well   nobody recommends thinking in those terms

so I place no question mark at the end

* * *

       see my therapist
       outside   already know more about him
              than I knew about other therapists I saw for years
take this to be a sign of his
mastery of the form
         you find a boundary you USE IT   lean against

a building with my shitty coffee   he moves in a slow
and generous way   so I allow time   for whatever his routine may be
sip
   sip   K asks me if I get jealous of his other patients   I say clients and she says
no we are
     patients   ok well no I don't   even consider that there are others

      I already know
      I'm going to complain about the people on the 6
the large woman who positioned her body   so everyone had to
    squeeze by her   she giving the eye   to everyone
I could barely contain my impulse
to tell her YOU ARE BRINGING THIS ON YOURSELF

changing your POV by a half degree

               can change your whole world

SHE IS HAVING EXACTLY THE EXPERIENCE SHE WANTS TO HAVE

     physical contact with great

               umbrage!

    there is no annoyance
without significance   daunted by the ways

    I'm authoring my own suffering   in the manner of families
lineages
      namesakes
         she who didn't have the heart to call me
             ANASTASIA
with the last name she had to take

    …she and three female servants were arrested and told to sacrifice to idols
        when they refused the three servants were put to death
           and Anastasia was burnt alive…

I could read martyr stories all night   what a charge
             // \\
      "women who gave their lives for the church"
             // \\
   in an everyday theology   *who knows? not me I never lost control*

                                    / / \ \
                              I am Antonin Artaud
so in love
                    I had a heart tattooed on my inner arm

          but it too is Christian   template comes from temple
                              spreadsheet comes from
                                        arranging psychic data

therapist
    asks
          what I love   about my job   he's not hearing it

under the complaint   OH! kick into
anaphoric speech pattern   beginning with I LOVE...

                                    * * *

                                                  coconut oil was solid this morning
my physician had said to keep doing what I'm doing   scoop the oil
into my coffee   K has no spare empathy   for faux medical freak-
                  outs   so summon my ex   my closest friend these days

I took   "your psyche is a Philip Guston painting"   as a compliment

          what sadists email   blood panel results   at 4am

left arm swells
      with mosquito bites
            find and easily kill it   smearing a thin horizontal blood
line
      when will it end?   it's true
             I'm "Head and Bottle 1975"
my low cholesterol
was a quiet point of pride   fuck you one can be fat AND healthy   a result

shattered my dawn   "don't worry there's a whole industry to help you"

      riddled uptown C ride   did I leave the door open
             oven on
                candle lit
  ABBY NORMAL
          sea foam green gown

did every email I send contain
misinformation   my physician says you have to know
      how to interpret their results   these results are astonishingly good!
your HDL level was
high and now it is even higher   what are you doing!?   well   I drink more
and eat more
meat   I lift
weights   she is
pleased   she speeds
through a list of
symptoms   me : wait wait wait   wanting to orate

about every part of my   body   before   it   flies   into

                        into pieces

* * *

shirt soaking in bathroom sink

hesitate   then brush teeth in kitchen   someone   who?

    said never to do this   my mother   something   about

Sicilians washing up at the kitchen sink

  K at clinic with Sunday hours for glue ear   common in kids

probably therapists too

        was hard to wake   a glass of peppery Spanish

wine   a jigger of a smooth sweeter bourbon   T came over with a chicken

watched *The Exorcist*   I remember   every possession

    scene like the back of my hand   the writing on my own stomach

but nothing of the theme of Damien the Greek son

    feeling so guilty for   his mother's death   of course the devil would

use her   and of course Damien says   "take me

        take me"

    my grandmother just phoned   I saw the movie at her

house when I was young   this means it would have been on TV   which seems

improbable   and that she let me watch it   improbable   nevertheless   this is how

    I remember my first viewing of *The Exorcist*   I feel guilty that I hate talking

    to her

so I answered   someone I think my father   told her

I have a hard time   with her breakdowns   she says   "I want you to know

        I think I'm over my depression and

crying phase"   what a shit

but don't take me   I say it's alright to cry   but a contingency is already

    understood   with this person   it is NOT alright for SOME people to cry

like it's not alright to lay around in bed   this morning I had

    to lace up my boots   having no plans to go   anywhere

but the kitchen table   where this is all happening

    my hair speaks   wildness   in the absence

    of behavior   on being childless   you find your

    children in all sorts of places

    both of my nephews are like me

in ways   but the one who never stops talking   I want to be like him

*   *   *

    in a constant struggle to keep

    a productive daily ritual

    I read a book on the daily rituals

of great writers   only several of them poets

    a key factor in greatness is not having

a job   other than writing   this handbook cannot teach me

    how to live

but I throw caution to the wind   :   take a pill to sleep   wake at 6am

drink 2 pots of coffee   catch up   on world news   then write for 4 hrs

sitting in bed smoking   with a box of donuts

    before meeting my lover   also a poet

    for early lunch   we discuss the movie we saw last night

then walk home   about 20 mins   but I stop in my favorite shops

and cafés so it takes longer   and I stop to jot my ideas   in a notebook
read for 2 hrs   at home   with pencil in hand
    correspondence   1 hr
        see friends for supper   one is my publisher
drink a bottle of wine   meet my other lover at the movies
    come home   strip
caress my breasts in front
    of a full length mirror   to get in touch with my powers
        to pick up the thread from morning   I write again
                                                for 2 more hrs

        bathe   sip tea and bourbon
listen to anything Puccini   my head wrapped
in a hot towel   lights out   at 11pm
                                        "and so it goes on
                                                day after day"

*   *   *

dad prepping car for Road America
March of Dimes race   March of Dimes   aims to improve the health
                                        of mothers and babies
        my mom says you know
your father   he has to show off his   skills   I'm sweating but won't
take off my denim
jacket   it's mid-October   dressed for an average   listening to a poet read

    last night in the parish hall   a line about rain   as we listened to it pour through 3 large windows open behind him

     it happens all the time   in the parish hall   mention a cat and a cat
will walk in from the garden

          the door having been propped   for air

every 5 minutes my grandma repeats that she didn't like

       when my grandpa drank   this was before I was alive

   I'm not surprised   he did give me my first sips   he said pulls
of beer   that crew partied   the Poles   in a family photo

   Uncle Ben   whose name was Ambrose

     is dressed as Peter Pan   he dropped a roast on his foot that night
and went to the ER

     my grandpa is Myra Breckinridge   my dad is in a diaper Baby New
Year   my Mom has a sash that says MS. POLAND   Halloween 46 years ago

    I wonder if I have ever had more fun

        fun is in my blood   I say outrageous things
dress up my speech every day   in overstatement   is when I feel closest
to my gods   Uncle Ben taught history at my high
school everyone was afraid of him but I knew

          he was Peter Pan   he said not to worry
I would never have to be in his class   but he was the best teacher of history
there was   so I didn't feel lucky   instead I got the woman who taught WWII
leaving out the Holocaust
and took leave with nervous exhaustion   I didn't like when Mike drank

    my grandpa whose name was Conrad
my physician just asked about my heart   history   I said my grandpa had his first heart

      attack when he was in his 50s   he must've smoked   no
but I just learned he did   socially

he read poetry   when he died in his bathroom
a morning in March 2002 there were books there   in particular
a copy of *The Granite Pail*   and Thomas Merton
                    I always set my watch   a minute ahead
representing a wish to have 60 seconds of
foreknowledge   an un-poetic advantage   when I'm in the parish hall
            I come to trust my senses   again   when people are worried
about the room not being big enough   the room turns in my head
        and I say don't worry   it's going to be just right
"look outside and you see it's middle night. Fucking ghosts crop up through the
windows"
            a line from Steve Benson's *Blue Book*
walking to meet Sue I took Atlantic   a way to the bar I never take
            and there I saw an old man and a Great Pyrenees
        at a table of books   flash of familiar cover   pale yellow of Godfrey's *Midnight
On Your Left*   alerted me
to poetry   and there   were many rare others I bought for $1 each
    I like to imagine writers in their surroundings   Steve says he was in his place
Mission district of San Francisco   I am in my bed   on a Sunday   desperate to extend
            time   dog snoring   yesterday I was
        exhausted from worrying about people
got dressed up   my blazers are tight
 in the shoulders   and arms   the focus of my weight lifting   because
really my arms are   what I have to see the most   extended out
        before me   hunting and pecking   then couldn't leave the house
    then fell asleep   watching   a horror movie   I saw when I was
so impressionable   I knew every affect   of that vampire
            think of Laura "I'm hammering Halloween

decorations   above the door"   being truly interested in her investment
in decorating   due to her use of the word "hammering"
I just threw out my plastic bloody slip-on finger
                    when I cleaned my desk in September   unprofessional sleight
of hand   tricking people visiting your office
into thinking you've had a workplace
            accident   let's summon   Winnicott   all we fear has already gone down
        yet there I was under the piano in one intern's leopard print baseball hat
drinking another intern's bourbon   sometimes a list of demands
and a list of mistakes is
the same list

* * *

pouring two cups of coffee into Polish
            stoneware   spilling one on bare thigh
during pivot toward table   pink boxers and white tank
stains as a first concern   alas   an ice pack   is needed
        T smells like roses   I don't want to tell the story
of why the first aid kit   is in Milwaukee   we go to the drugstore
something that still exists   on the corner   for burn cream and nonstick pads
            a honey bee lands on her hand and won't leave by force of air
it all seems charmed   for two people
having a hard time   once when John dropped something in this kitchen   he said
MUST RE-ASSOCIATE   I wrote off the possibility of any real damage
to my flesh   a psycho fantasy   set right by a weeping blister

* * *

read aloud 25 pages of latest Susan Howe   "the telepathy
of the archive"   its insistence that you have to be there   to get the extent
of the message   revel in mom's statement
                that she forgot to call on Sunday
                                                she may be lying
                                        but that too would be wonderful
                                                to figure out someone's attachment
can be more fluid than you thought   that is wonderful for each person
                she told me that my nephew   learned about Van Gogh
and his ear   she asked him if he knew what he did
                with   his ear   after
                he   cut   it   off   knowing he wrapped it in paper   took it to a brothel
he said   duh   grandma   he put it in a memory box

                "your heart's not in it"   said a friend   and I balk
        but wait
        what's my heart in?   oh bother   DUH   in my pocket

"A glass of papaya juice
and back to work" (O'Hara)   see the genius composer   walking on the avenue
where he has a place   he really is nice
                        I tell my therapist   I have to think of him more
                what with my lack of monster   skin
I jump up from the leather recliner

and impersonate   someone not nice   their meanness seeped in muscle
memory   so easy for me   to call forth   how do you impersonate kindness?
    or is it so nourishing it's absorbed   doesn't need to be expelled through
                                    gestures

                            *   *   *

happy place : Stacy is walking
in the woods with her hounds this misty Wednesday morn
        after a third restless night
composing mental memos   the judge   vs.   the diplomat
all I want for Christmas   is my two front teeth
                    the only person who is really indispensible
        at this moment   is me   Love, Me
    phone is bright at 4am   hope the person next to me
        will not wake   as she has to wake in 2 hours
to catch a flight   read an article on phone
                about age being a state of mind   when environments of seniors
when they were in their primes   the 1950s   are simulated
and they live in the experiment
they even HEAR better after awhile   their GRIPS are more firm   AND
        people guess that they are younger   much like being
unable to process death   I am unable
                to process that it is no longer the 1980s
I am simulating my fantastical 80s   young men
who box   running at night   in the chill   smell barrels
of burning leaves   stout dykes playing cards

look at my pitch black hair   I understand French
and   wear parachute pants   I hang out in a garage   or an attic
        or a back porch   so many spaces to choose from!   I know
what I'm becoming   butch   and that I will always need this
to hear better   and for my grip   plus some women who appreciate me
        and a little antipathy   coming from

                                                wherever

                              * * *

dog's ball not under couch
peer over balcony and see a blue smudge in the courtyard down
4 flights   Grey is sick   no meeting
            a vast connectivity problem   I imagine   a thick chartreuse
cloud over the metropolis   Boerum Hill   the East Village   I don't mind the effect
of slowing work down   but I am impatient with impediments   Green Slime
            K calls from LA   I am drinking good coffee alone
        she is drinking bad coffee in the sludge of family home
it's a *Foxbase Alpha* morning   into afternoon   weather in the Palisades
        closer to body temp   a heat wave   St. Etienne   making "Only Love
Can Break   Your Heart"   danceable
in my navy cloak   splitting a sweet potato with the dog
            head a bit of an ache from last night's
        excessive smudging   text from neighbors   "NO JUDGEMENT BUT
are you smoking pot?   just want to make sure someone didn't break into
        our apartment   and smoke pot"   oh no   I'm performing
a ritual cleansing over here   which brings me to my dream neighbor

swimming in swirling Arctic ice pools with a polar bear
                some sense of danger from bear attack   drowning   or freezing
                        current pushes me against what looks like a manmade
            wall   a simulated wall for climbers   I hold on
            elk   walk by with each step forward they   transform   into
                            more muscular   healthier looking   elk
they step forward but forward means into the past   today's elk are thin
        they step forward into their robustness   before the catastrophe   in case
there was any doubt neighbor   :   today's   elks are thin

        my head aches even after fresh air
and good coffee   Italian for beginners   at 12:45   been thinking
        of what I'll say when asked why I'm taking the class   well I'm half Italian
well no   Sicilian actually   you know   that area   and I love
this poet Pasolini and want to   um Nov. 2 is the 50th anniversary
of his unsolved murder   and I think about
                that often   that no one has solved this man's murder
            T brought me a second copy of *Divine Mimesis*
        with Leslie's ex libris stamp   pages are falling out of my copy
I put them next to each other   one Italian lesson in Chicago and several
Arabic   headache worse post-Stefano   "flirt
                with Zoraida   I say that because your speaking is angular
seduce her!"   wait is he acknowledging that I'm the queer here or
do Italians just want to seduce everyone with their musicality?

        "repeat after me" MOLTO BENE!

* * *

6:30 on a Tuesday near the end of the 10th month
        is dark   I nearly walk into a man sitting on the sidewalk
        in front of the poorly lit park   many things this fall are
           on   Tuesdays   my dog duty night
tonight I would've liked to hear Kim Lyons and John Godfrey read

yesterday when I heard that I won a prize I could have
        saved a baby from a burning ca.   I could have walked on the walls of the office
FEEL MY HEART   and bless the..   Nicole and Laura did

        how have I written in this state   the state is the form the love takes
I pull it off
             flashback to the huddle   my brother drawing the play
          in his palm   receiver always   because his friends couldn't tackle me

        today I smelled those rubber bait worms   then a tray of
            toasted buns   from my fast food job

        I'm also missing the screening of "Blue Tape"   and a panel on comedy
and art   a young man on the F was wearing an outfit
        very me   self-consciously   adjusting his belt   his
sleeves   his long bangs   which touched my hand which was holding the
            pole   when he looked down at
         his shoes   he sniffed his armpit   I'm right up
    on him and I can't smell him   but perhaps this is the dawn

of the dulling of my senses   or I only smell the past   I can no longer make out
            the Poetry in Motion poem   just the title   "Scaffolding"
with that title the poem doesn't even need to happen

9:45 on Halloween morning   ate an apple   checking for razor blades
                was all the rage   in my neighborhood   sit in a shallow bath
        to ease cramps   only lasts for 2 days now
                    tonight   met with Grey   "yo mentor"   we talk
  about Pasolini   and how I can make myself a man through
the multiplication of presents   it works for me   Grey and I   2 men
            in 2 days a gay genius will be massacred
        somewhere   and a passerby will think
            is that a pile of rubbish?   that is the continual present of finding
                Pasolini's body in Ostia   1975

4pm the bells of St. Agnes
            make me feel like I'm in another country   they are tinny
don't sound like recordings   I can only conjugate 2 verbs
in Italian   stare and essere   possibilities for restructuring myself
            singular and plural   Stefano starts filling in my homework
ugh   the look of a dullard
        I didn't sleep well last night
                        the wind howling through the a/c   outdoor
        furniture   slamming   about
                        "HURRY UP PLEASE IT'S TIME"   a wonderful
line   I remove

the a/c   water pours onto my rain boots   HAR HAR
can of garbanzos smacks onto the balcony and rolls into the planter
HAR HAR   it's daylight savings   and all the devices have auto-aligned   then
there are my 4 anarchist wrist watches   in a rankle over the year

* * *

why should they have believed in me
they never heard of such a thing
not even a plan   but an invitation to keep the faith
with a poet   lean all of my weight to open
the iron-trellised door
of my therapist's building   I thought it was I
who was in danger   but it's my partner with
an abnormal result   I'm being punished   for winning something
therapists   find this fascinating   but how could I
write   if I believed in randomness?

"we are all
in danger"   (Pasolini)   I try the deity ring
on pointer finger   clearer of obstacles   therapist
suggests I meet malicious magic   on its own terms
with benevolent magic   I believed my friend would conceive
holding my hand   after a dinner of rare duck and wine
a hopeful gesture when   even women in Italy are having
fewer babies   austerity measures   2 of my elders
talk about the end   at the hands of billionaires

therapist and I talk   about Jesus indeed
    finding what I sought   has left me troubled
has not yet given way to wonder   a still boat in the
doldrums of the Atlantic   I try
to embroider

        a new universe   with new information

                    an act of ear-driven

    translation

                        * * *

I'm not gonna crate the dog
gonna need him in the night   when my motor starts to overheat
run one hand along the edge of the bed   one upon another breed of mammal
                this is me metabolizing
        group trauma   what I bring to the company
is shit don't stick to me   a mind not deranged from years   of knowing
the right thing   yet doing the wrong thing   therapist says AA
isn't everyone's cup of tea   but they really get the physiology
    I shake bitters into seltzer and pop the seal   on a Greek
yogurt   share it
with the dog   Tuesday dinner   it's not that I've never wanted
        to call a do-over   I regret the time I had words
with a neighborhood girl   then offered to shake
                        and make up   as I took her hand I put my foot
in her gut   fell backward   throwing her   over my head
            a move I learned in judo   pure disbelief   the look on her

face   that something like that could
                              happen in our world

                              *   *   *

fog reconstitutes   ability to do morning chores
     have to love my people extra hard
tins of tea   "hospitality" line item   supply all manner
     of container   "no time   to go to the rock shop"

he only howls   when he hears sirens   so   many
               times a day   the liver
boils over and put out the flame   while I made
     the bed   BE PANORAMIC   in your railroad   flat

one of the neighbor's bees   in bedroom   dog
               trying to catch it   I must take action   become
an activist   do I kill the bee?   humanity
can only live 4 years without them   no I don't kill the bee

skipped dinner   Italian   gym   stopped reading   a series
of deprivations   natural rhythm for my religion   during the awesome
dark   <u>glow worms</u>   <u>government house</u>   <u>safer rooms</u>
<u>obviously for the guiltiest</u>   things I underlined in the Sciascia book

before dust settled   upon it

"your bangs are ostentatious"   fights generate

retrospective humor   she wants me to say more   I want her

       to say less   "but you aren't changing!"

                Rome wasn't built in a day

* * *

Thich Nhat Hanh critical

      in Plum Village   I brown the sausage   take it easy

before 9am   attended 4 hour meeting yesterday

   was 10 minutes   late   didn't note between 10th and 11th which had

       me traversing half the island   surely they will supply coffee

 a voluntary Sunday   morning meeting   everyone on the F

had roller bags

       no coffee

    I'm a lousy participant   maybe partly why   yesterday

  I quit Italian   I have perverse   timing

opening my mouth   just in time to get   cut off   no time

    for homework   too depleted to go to class

"being an ED is the hardest

 job in the world"   someone at the meeting

     said   oh.

          stop into Revolution Books   small poetry section has titles by

     Robert Pinsky   I said   there is nothing harder

to raise money for than poetry

        ensemble group on train   "I won't be afraid

                as long as you   stand by me"

          *   *   *

one friend reminds me   chest pains   can be stress
another if I don't get back to the gym   by January I'll be depressed
during Q & A   someone asked me how I decide
what to put in/what to leave out   the National Book
Awards really missed an opportunity this year   looking back at our nation
in 2014   grand jury still out in Ferguson   not giving it to *Citizen*
poetry has a power   that must be isolated from the people   there are always plenty
who will say it's dead   on cue   a nation that knows the right thing
but consistently does the wrong thing   that's a sick mind   Allan
Kornblum passed away this morning   he used to lunch with me
when he came to NYC   we'd meet at Veselka   he'd share his excitement
about new Coffee House titles   and talk about Ben Franklin   I started to
       think of him as Ben Franklin

                     what I decide to put in

                        is writing   as in I don't
know what I think   till I'm writing   gets me out of the limits of obsession

where I just spin my wheels into a truck sized grave   I wanted this fragrance
the store only had a new tester so I negotiated half price   button up
light blue shirt   and walk into puff of herbal mist   my heart is pounding
    Monday   Monday   Monday   my phobia about possessing 5 out of 5

qualities of unhappy people   Paul and I   walking the dog   passed a statue
which I point out   "oh   sexy Jesus"
NO! different wound pattern   that's St. Sebastian   later he texts
me a picture of a painting of St. Sebastian   "SEXY JESUS"

* * *

helicopter   hovers   above my neighborhood   streets
are quiet   staring at my dog on a Tuesday night   eat a meatball
pour bourbon   reading   a history of the Black Panthers
watch videos of friends stopping traffic   which crises
will be a healing crisis?   left the house wearing my school
colors   not in the mood for this train car   every man with legs spread
was hanging on by 3 threads   now I'm in the wind   there are documents
I bared to look at once   have 4 days
to reconstitute   in the gaseous container of mob mentality   favored
by poets of the aristocracy   make a meal   give thanks
that I have myself   my material life
end of the Black Panthers book   the authors explain
why revolutionary movements don't exist anymore   in the United States

* * *

I used to like the holidays more   when I had a familiar place to return to
I'm untethered   snow crunches under my feet
we're figuring it out   going out to dinner is nice   everyone

is cute   and polite   hot pie   I have a scotch drink   bartender lights the
          orange peel   I talk about how
I still consider myself a Christian   interested in the teachings of Christ
          Smith St. is so barren   I run down the center   then it hits me   a sore throat
laying all plans   to rest   get upright   4 days later
          a white beard hair   visit to urgent care   where a doctor
takes 2 seconds   to diagnose infection

* * *

helicopter wakes me at 6am
hovering above the block for ages
Dec. 4 the FBI
murders Fred Hampton
my routes feel the same   head in a drain
spinning for relevant politics
Eric Garner's last words   an illuminated history book
St. Agnes programmed   their bells   a Christmas
tune   sunset on the roof   throw ball to dog
from plastic lounger   each   day   passes and feels like   life has changed
same food stares back at me from the fridge   buy another
scarf to layer over other scarf   then sit
shunning all social activity   in my scarves
slip some brain cells   into the joy of Miriam
Makeba's
"every Friday and Saturday night it's   Pata Pata time"
she wished another song had become her hit

                    because this one didn't mean anything
                              Live in Paris version on repeat   "it is now
            that I must
            set the stage
for that spectacular success which must
animate   my later days"
                                    where once I thought of ditching
            the city   now it seems unethical   to regret
      life   which   ditching the city would mean   to me
                  O'Hara said he felt more
            adventurous each time
      his heart
      was broken   seems so whimsical this day in December   as does the red heart
            spray-painted   on the shield of the St. Mark's lion   what do we feel
when   our hearts   are broken by an ill too large
                  to grasp
            I am willing to try
      new methods of engagement   my heart on my shield

                              *   *   *

one of my roots   is so subterranean
                              survival was impossible   one of them still moves
      with a wide wag
                        took out the garbage   four-story trail of leakage
whole building smells   like gingko berries   life might be easier

114

if we decided to do things badly

which is to say it smells
like vomit   my neighbor
                    says "rowdy party on 3 last night"   thinking
        my garbage was their party   the stuff of infamy!   PUKERS!

DOUCHE BAGS!   it all started when I threw out   coffee grounds
pork chop bones   some arugula   a cheese rind...

        drink tea in morning dark   today's work
requiring   Black Sabbath
             Paris 1970

in 7th grade I was etching   Scorpions   into the desk   Cheap Trick

not knowing Ozzy's hotness   was waiting to reveal itself to me over 30 years later

        wish I smoked   I would go to the courtyard   the cigarette facilitating

meditative omens
in dead scrub   I wish I could admin   pain
                    away   my therapist refers to my work
camp   the one I run on the inside   I tell him the ZEK
        of my name is   a Russian slang term for inmate

when I walk by the fast food place on 1st   also in my image   old women
        sitting one to a table   sipping from foam cups

a Vulnerable Person alert vibes my phone   I am in charge
        and this is what   I dream up for the future
                                        home late   from a reading
K from the bed   "do you celebrate anything" uh
                                                    oh
        I've travelled far on quickness to laughter   "does anything mean anything
                                                    to you?"
                                        anything
                                                    besides poetry
        I think she means   like a holiday   and no —
                                        suggests today   St. Lucia
Day   can't deny we could use   a festival
of light   bringing together Scandinavia   and   Italy   of course
                                        they emphasize different aspects
        of her story   we go with Scandinavia   bake cookies
and read Donne
                "Send forth light squibs
                                            no constant rays

        The world's whole sap is sunk...   I, by Love's limbec, am the grave

                                        Of all   that's nothing"

* * *

he carried 3 small   xmas trees
by their necks like   dead rabbits
            path in front of church narrowed   by tree-seller
                    plus annoyance of the locked main gate   get elbowy   bow
out of the secret santa   would have preferred buying cookies
        from DiRobertis   GONE   when you know something about a story
and you watch CNN report on that story   there's the boot in the face
        effective mind-control   sometimes even the minds of poets
                    intrusions to writing leave me
            short on words   there is something important
        I should be doing right now   Roberto used to call writing on the job
"a victory for poetry"   so many people get rude this month I'm always
on   as a daddy
saw a famous guy   after he was a dick
to me   taking the F   he looked in rough shape   I smiled
I still love you   man
    even though you don't know   who I am
            and never will

* * *

the line for the reading is out to 10th
            see a photo of it later that night   what strange light
        church's façade harkens   an old schoolhouse   or the farm

when it was Bowery No. 1   after scamming land from the Lenape
        we are gathered here today
                        trust no high and mighty lord of land   "we are gathered
        during this time of incarnation"   roving singers   a pine wreath
                for language in wondrous   manner
                                                last week's poet   David Antin   began
        "I can see Paul Blackburn laying on the floor with his tape recorder"
                visions of Paul making an archive   beneath the floor
                                                        is inwood
                                                marble pompton
                                                        soil

                        I read it as
                during this time of incarceration
        tonight   Rankine's *Citizen*   Jarnot's "Every Body's Bacon"
a poet walking up the steps turned and said   "thank you
        for the space   and I mean not just the room"

                                * * *

work late Friday before holiday break   cans of worms
open rather than close   real anxieties plus one paranoid
wormhole   drink pumpkin ale neighbors left in the hall
after party   peer out window to see if mailbox on corner is still
there   one on Smith welded shut   mail LOI to a poetry foundation
everyone is prone to infighting   even now that we can read
the COINTELPRO papers   crinkling sound in my jacket is a sweet note
from K which I forgot was there   take dog to his

favorite place   where DeGraw dead ends at the canal   jowls and ears
to the ground crazed by a scent   Ted calls 10:30am on a Saturday "were you asleep?"
no just in bed   "I thought you were 24/7"   headache from lack of water
and feasting from a jar of gummy candy   kinds I didn't even know existed!
on roof with erica and T as they
smoked in the cold night   couldn't re-associate   get out of work space
K sleeping after double session with a patient   I've over-
taken her sugar intake   as if together we need sugar
look at red grooves at my waist and shoulders   six weeks
of stress eating   do crunches at the gym   this is rock bottom
the note lives in my pocket   I crinkle the paper with my hand
it's a stadium coat   some have said an Olympic diver keeping warm
coat   a Russian coat   a mob coat   it all pleases me   Jen calls
hers a stadium coat   run into her on Court with my dog   going to
pick up her dog   I'm a marble being pulled to the center   THE PROBABILITY
OF AN EVENT BEING DETERMINED BY SUMMING
TOGETHER ALL THE POSSIBLE HISTORIES OF THAT EVENT
an infinity of this   pleases me   just as I   being a writer in NYC
am pulled to the center   where the large object creating the dimple
is a massive amount of biography   similarly my brother and I don't call
each other   my relationship with him has occurred is occurring and will occur
with effort set forth in the 70's   LA in December is reincarnation   high tops
        on muscle beach   return to the party from the roof
"Paul says you would never do karaoke"   it is nice to be known by Paul
what else would I never do   hang glide?   nothing high risk
Paul says "you take them in your writing"   we burst into laugher
then I head out to find   the G just after midnight

WINTER

this dog needs a yard   jogging with him
                                  act of pure love

10:20am seniors pour
 out of St. Agnes   Roman
                              Catholic church   I don't want to go
to LA or any-
where since
my first dog
died on a road trip   the new me

    wed   to routine   in a cultural capital   go into every Italian
deli and bakery   for a mile on Court   looking for pignoli and fresh
 mozzarella   none

of the guys call me "sis"
       like they did at Glorioso's

run to Tony's
for a key   FOR LEASE
no groceries and now no hardware
family who owns American Beverage   posts closing sign
nothing to drink

* * *

it's good to have coffee the way you like it
      most strange Christmas   Venice
                          Hollywood a movie
we didn't want to see but the time was right   in Los Feliz
        Santa Monica where on Wilshire
only a deli was open   brisket and matzo ball

    soup to-go   nothing on cable   at a stand still
               as far as inventing   a new
tradition   talked to mom on street corner
              she had words with her mom   "another down

day"   my book for the trip   *Ned Rorem's Paris*
    and New York Diaries   untouched   underlined from the
intro weeks back   "clarifies our ragout" and "community
    is hard to come by"

the city I came back to   NYPD
    regarding the mayor as a public enemy
aggression ravages the top layer
which is   the lie
             no one I know had a good year

New Year's Eve   every one

   says 2015 has to be better   I'm alone on my couch

                  too tired to party

   Paul texts "can't wait till you

have a different job   and can be normal"   eating cold leftovers

slightly abject and in the home

   true to my astrology   can't pay attention to a decent movie

      but that's how

                    an anti-pleasure system   works

       pro-exhaustion

           a toast!   let's be better

              editors

I'll chart

my mutiny   pro-scrutiny   a toast!

let's not let our ties erode

outside our media

       a toast!   those whose actions I can't comprehend

           because trauma looks different

            on everyone

a toast!   "that we come into a wide

      space of heart   and hearts"   (Baraka)

* * *

by the end of the   night

I didn't   want   the bread   or   the champagne

the coffee   or the cake

leave all leftovers   my job is done

I have been thanked   with a few trinkets   a stone

to absorb negative energy

a tampon   encrusted in purple beads   a few told me

that they remember that I am a person   with feelings

some performances

grounded me

New Year's Day feeling either unreal   or an eternal present

poets hurling

into the trash all dates   which have no resonance in our spirit

thinking of Gramsci's   "I Hate New Year's Day"

this is our township   lacking its usual troubles   feels unreal

but still   some will always have the bravado

to complain   to show that they

are in pain   which must be at the root   I love how they

annoy me   their mini-manifestos

our elders were not silly   to think of scope

the power to include   means say yes till you can't

* * *

after some gynecological surgeries   they'll tell us
we can go back to work   right away   so when we're laid up we feel
like we're the only woman among women   who cannot return directly to work
"it must be me"   is a feeling that can't be inspired too much   in social control
I suggested my friend   take 2 days off   she's home
with a heating pad   I bundled up   said goodbye
to the dog   then sat on the couch
and didn't move   last night's event   well I should
have a lot to say   today   but I'm like a bear in the "feels like" nothing degree
air   feels like nothing
metabolism   a hunk of amber in my gut

* * *

air matches my hair   salt and pepper   salt being
           snow
           pepper being dust
maybe we'll be remembered

as poetry roadies   insane podium
       needs a scrub

      "Tuesday peut-'être?"   want to get together? yes!

long live the system
  of informal mentorships
        it may be impossible
       to shed
        your first public
       identity   you could drive
       a thousand miles then
         walk a block
when pressed
my resolution
      is to stretch
         each morning   must understand
"open hips"
    pain at the desk   wearing the hell outta the black tee

I got

in LA

        over Christmas borscht   Bob

     said   it comes down to setting the room

the solid citizen archetype

  or the ruler   whose desire is control   the magician

who knows that moving each chair an inch   this way

             or that

    could make or break a dream

* * *

   a US head-of-state addresses the French people   in FRENCH

            John Kerry

               first time since FDR

               1942 over Radio-London

a quarter of the United Nations attend a solidarity march   NOT US

     I smell pine

     in the movement of air

     after throwing on my coat

is it a good sign or bad

or worse

no sign   there isn't a street that isn't

         lined with discarded pines

"is it all over my face?"

        in front   of the wrought iron door   take a picture
of my face   wrought iron hair   buzz   Tuesdays fear
the weight of my body
won't suffice
  and I will have to   buzz
               a second time

therapist   "most can't get by on as little as you can"

but … but…
     I can show you how to thin
            your gruel   just ask!

move *Intimate Journals* on top of *Indian Journals*
beside *The Journalist*
            a neglected human right
the freedom to make and remake
        ourselves and our cities   today is the fourth
               day   I have not shit
               on anyone's dreams

and I feel fine   after 9/11 Jim Hodges asked
     UN delegates to write   "don't be afraid" in the language

of their country for a mural   the only country
        to formally refuse

                                    yes
                                    the US

                    *   *   *

            recall on proper names
                slower   panic
                get crossword
            magazine "challenging"
                I'll be a person
            who does crosswords
        can't figure out a single clue

            deep inside I'm short
                on continuity
            yesterday didn't happen
            there is no tomorrow
            and I'm not gathering
                rosebuds either

                I'm just doing
            my job   staying out
                of trouble

* * *

picking up food to cook for the dog on 2nd "chicken livers!

  chicken livers!" a woman is delighted following me

 "young lady you reminded me
    that I want chicken livers!"

* * *

"Here is the newsflash ——'

  Bad news coming," *1984*

       the paranoid-schizoid position of the earliest months of an
    infant's life no integration between good or bad the projection
      of badness

someone get me a theory of healthy action using all powers of body and mind

a despot King Abdullah of Saudi Arabia is dead

President Obama

is going to that funeral skipped the Paris unity rally one being crucial   the other optional   there are

work groups   and failed work groups   those that crumble

                                            into assumption

                              *   *   *

grateful to lay back in
5 inches of hot water
dusk must be a good time
for the boiler   historic storm   horrible fallacy of the present   spewing
from the radio   I guessed I was 6 for
that storm in April   but I was 4   it was the drifts that made it
historic   an event I can verify online   don't know what's really happening
or   who exactly is on the streets
in the shadows of a "driving ban"
while in here it's blankety and bingey
on drama   pack the crack   in my forehead with anti-aging
cream   part of me wanting to keep visible the difficulties
of women between 40 and 50   of which
this crack is born   and sometimes splits like a dry thumb
effort at "cow face" ritual   also half-hearted   involving holding an under bite
and looking to the stars
one of few habits ever quickly formed   TV
anything healthier makes me feel guilty for not working   such as
how can I stretch my back   when my inbox has an overcrowding problem?

honing a new mid-look   lesbian Depardieu
still the desire
to reign in the field
of poet self-portraiture   an endeavor
to imbue my figure with something it lacks
or never had at all
turbulent world   buy another Swatch in Union Station
DC   almost the weekend   when I get that inconsolable look
around 2:30pm   Sunday   and ask "is it time?"
although today is January 30th and the month has lingered
the Swatch is a combo of camouflage and white flowers with gold numerals
reminding me of a Jim Hodges piece
said to the woman who wanted me to try it on   no can you ring it up fast
I have a train to catch   she shrugged her shoulders
to rip time off the charts I need the time piece
I'm an easy human to track but my crimes
are never going to entail being
on the lam
so with abandon   post pictures of
Baltimore // Newark // Philly
out the train window
text my ex   hey I'm passing through

4:30am sound of sleet   this one looks more menacing
        for the pedestrian   but with less media tadoo   mere advisory
stare at the pot of cream   should I just throw away the fern
    I used to talk to   set near the oxalis   it's not like
I suddenly stopped believing in plant communication   new cactus clippings
now join in   my baser impulses funneled   you're coming into
        the bedroom   the office isn't clear cut
    as a sanatorium   it gets grim in here

* * *

dream : can't button my favorite blue shirt   shoulders too broad   I look
for a tailor for hunchbacks   got grant check yesterday   pay Master
    Card   purchase canvas bag with a lifetime
warranty   what's a fetish again?   I just like bags
        remembering the East Village in 1995   Ken Schles
"I didn't want to walk around the neighborhood
  with my camera
by myself"   1995   a friend's empty apt. along Tompkins
        building manager called her to say "there's a man sleeping
    in your bed"   it was me   went back to Philly

dream : I'm imitating Joe Cocker   to entertain friends
        his greatest hit   the lyrics flow   it's a nonexistent
    song   I realize when I wake up   and try to find it online

carried that check for days   kinetic as a wallet   new phone tracks my
steps 8,000 today   my sedentary job takes me places
          next time something needs to be found
in the basement
 let it be me
          organizational memory
                how many times have you cracked your head
                on the cavern beam?

or was it a Bob
Seger hit?   one of those songs that was always playing while waiting
                in the back seat of a hot car for my mom while she picked
                up a few groceries

dream: I hire a craven event planner hereby known as   DRACULA
                                                for her single-minded pursuit of
                                                sponsorship cash

          I know all about vampires   some of you
                can turn yourselves
                into mist

                              * * *

white dog hair in my espresso   happy adoptiversary dude
daily reminders that progress   is not linear

over 200,000

people applied for   a one-way mission

to Mars

is this a 0 an 8 or a 9?

time these glasses get a string   the moon is the only

light I see   did Pope Francis

really say animals go to heaven?   or a mistranslation of this:

"…the fulfillment of this wonderful design also affects everything around us"

where is everyone?

no one responding to emails   fill out Amtrak survey so I can complain

about the intensity of heat   on the first leg of trip to DC

decide to go with pop tone banana split covers   last minute freak

out about usage of proper

names   become the poet who edits the poem while in proof

stage   replace 3 names   with pronouns   and maybe in

later editions I'll change them back

I'm SO sorry!   I make a joke so the editors know

that I know   I'm being   annoying

* * *

used to think just getting by day to day in New York City was accomplishment enough now
I'm failing harder at being unnoticeable with this monster bark coming from my house   if
I can situate myself in a landscape with humans I am not depressed so I take the dog to the
canal where there are workers and feral cats

therapist pointed out a grammatical error in my speech   says it must be bad if it has gotten
to the poets   I explain that poets don't care about grammar   I ask if this is
therapeutically relevant which he later remembers and wants to return to at my
convenience   grammar is very emotional   what I did was put myself first

it was revealed to me in a Christmas card that my grandmother claims a 7th sense which is
how she knows that she will never see me again no one knows what her 6th sense is or if she
has an 8th   who is the Pancreatic Patron Saint? there's the glorious wonder-worker St.
Peregrine who was healed of cancer   any Saint who forsook all the comforts of a life of
ease will do

thinking about that time tires me   like walking on a cold icy day trying not to slip   every
muscle tensed   how will I ever get from here to my desk in the East Village

* * *

such a rush
to get the 2,000 pages of Leopardi's notebooks   on onion skin
       all I've done is set my cup on it...

open to pg 741 : where an unhappy man is incapable
of compassion   flip to 804 : where it's difficult to know
           how to laugh about ordinary things

pg 1095 : *ermo* [solitary] *eremo   romito   hermite   hermitage   hermita*
and   fear
        is egotistical   each fears for himself during times of public
        misfortune

*   *   *

"our speakers don't have much time..."
David Carr dies that evening
                watch the video where he talks to Snowden   from
Russia   Greenwald
    and   Poitras   he coughs several times
        I have my rocks from the rock shop in one hand   scoffed at
thumping my chest but invest
                in blue apetite and smoky
                        quartz   the combo   who knows
    is just pleasing to clack
                in my fist

*   *   *

one email on President's Day   I guess
        people really aren't working
neighbors blasting bad pop
        long robe my dad gave me from a trip to Japan

25 yrs ago   and a knit hat   favorite winter
          ensemble   the email said   "off to Wall St. for divestment
day"   see commercial at gym   the only way the US can get ahead
          FRACKING
the newscaster so much less horrible than most
     I have a crush by the end
of my cardio   orange bag on yellow chair
          overcoming chromophobia as a way to grow
old   you have not made it until you can say   "I can't do it
                    I will be in Europe in May"
newscaster says ISIS

                         wants to kill
                    the pope   21 Copts
                    beheaded   in Libya

     my fear envisions forces that single me out   eye for an eye
          in my Italy   look into tour of tunnels
               of St. Callixtus   resting place   of popes

                              feeling at once
                              larger and
                              smaller
                              than I actually
                              am

* * *

        worse than the shoddy apartments available
           to the small nonprofit arts administrator
              was less room to think
guy whistles *Star Wars*
        theme waiting for the 6
            is crunching almonds on the train
          akin to nail clipping   the thought being too much
to bear   stops me   just as I could not risk
my back pack ever intruding upon another
        impeccable proprioception   down here   like it's going
          to rub off
next stop 2nd Avenue
        can be so emotional
         if somewhat communally produced
           I get off on 2nd Avenue   but till then I sit and think
   for the last minutes   of the ride
from Bergen   my thoughts
     ranging for infinite lessons   I sit on a seat and think
             by a window   with letters scratched into it

* * *

three hearts
triple threat

* * *

"I keep seeing used Borsalinos and
         thinking of you"   writes Diana   but I spent the money on other
accessories   I watched the dance with new sensitivity about where to look   the space
         was the problem   told Ariel I was going to learn "Trio A"
"like your body acquiring a rare book"   don't care how foolish I look my weak muscle
         memory   faintly signaling for it   all I've ever wanted
    from a group of friends is in Forti's "Huddle"   closest I ever came
was a pyramid in the graveyard   true for many groups   if they were
    to keep minutes   they'd find that the same meeting has been occurring
         for decades except sometimes the compensation   gets worse!
                              we keep a comprehensive bunker
to fuel the meeting of ages   every worthy statement auto-creating   its mnemonic
       the hawk visited us that day and let us see her binocular eye
now that is a highly organized system   for seeing risk
               shifting on my flattened tailbone wedge I tell the consultant
      about my "pain points"   the space is more of a problem than the dance
but let's see   do hawks always bring a message   we start the research
     line up the pieces   of dual-action apatite   I see a feminism
that doesn't disrupt self-care   all the body workers I need just to stand before you
tonight   I can see

how Agnes Martin   "left New York because of remorse"
"discovered to be missing" (Jill Johnston)   the sickest play on words a woman can
know   the remorse a woman takes in when no one else is capable of it?
    my church is an hour too   call each Sunday to the place of
such crescendo   70 year old mother caring for her mother   who whispers
    to her   "I know she broke your heart"   "I told her you are   where you belong"
        remorse with as many sunk   as in the Great Lakes   so I see dreaming
            desert literature   simply ocular   this first day of meteorological
spring   a metaphor for the start of better times   but spring is when warm air and cold
often meet   to create instability   Alexis built a primitive shelter   invited me
    to write for the oldest surviving lesbian literary   magazine
                                        asked me if I liked Agnes
        Martin   our worlds were never supposed to collide   I had never
heard of Moondog then suddenly Moondog   was everywhere
    I had never thought of T as an ecstatic   then suddenly she was beside
        herself and I   as her reader   beside myself   the tulips look bruised and alert
this morning   last night I saw my familiar   but still can't read her
maybe it is because of my paternity   that I cannot see a man catch a ball
        without choking up   in my play book it says   like Kenny Washington said
LIFT AS YOU CLIMB

* * *

fern is recovering in the bedroom
      I hold small fronds
   end of life planning   is important
        for *everyone*

                   said for my benefit
            13 years senior   that business card
               still kicking around

   the new show's hook
for me
   they live in a house

                guy at Park Natural admonishes me
          for sniffing soap   I once climbed
        a picnic table bench
           to pick an unripe plum
        scolded by a Roman Catholic
           a plum worth a girl's confidence

covered in his winter
white hair   make note
   take him in for dew claw

grown circular   growled
at me   the other night
noli me tangere

                job shifting into deep thinking
                    it looks like I've gone cryogenic
                        hand Simone the yellow stone

wake up my solid stomach
still upset   a formal concern

ethics of believing our souls choose
our parents   the stomachs
we deserve

                      because I didn't go   to grad school
                        I guess   I had not envisioned tables
                    my friend the professor told me they
                      get confessional   one asks "are you
                                      butch?"

      1 through 6 trains delayed today
      3 Gs go by before the F
        it's even snowing down here
through the vent   where I'm waving
the phone above my head
to catch a signal

                              criminality as explanation   or   a planet
                                                            disappearing
                                                            an airplane

LBJ asked
what if you gain the whole world
    and lose your own soul?
        from the bible
        ended his speech
            with "we shall
                overcome"

                                        sometimes it takes the anniversary
                            of a death   to feel   the person join the
        other dead in you   a table of those who talk and those who just sit
                            there and make faces   Akilah talks

student says she notices the women
        they're reading "call out the poem"
mentioning the poem in the poem
            April 1st will be one year
                and I will say goodbye to this poem

* * *

you don't have to

remember to spring

ahead   devices do it

6:04pm the room is golden

salmon in the oven   parents say they're sending a letter

where everything is   in case they die

together unexpectedly   Monday 9am meeting

psychic stone in the shoe   what I like about lifting weights

visible results   plus the dream of becoming a power lifter   spend hours

online searching for the right shoe   something Italian

and expensive   my watch has slipped   face rests on my inner wrist

how the priests   when they let me be an altar boy   would wear them

when they lifted their arms to praise God   to glance at the time

and preserve an illusion   of divinity   the landlord posted another sign

about door mats

being a violation of fire code   everyone needs to remove

their bikes   or he will   mine is a rusted sky blue frame

at the reading everyone said what they were looking

forward to when the snow melted   *riding bikes*

everywhere!   I made something up not wanting to let on that I was born

into an inability   to "look forward"   one poet was so close to me I couldn't read her

face   it was in a house requiring that I take my shoes off to enter

violating my code of preparedness   getting ready to go   I had asked K how I looked

"like a middle-aged

lesbian with avant-garde
leanings"

        is perfectly accurate   *don't ever say that again*   throwing off the black
flannel cape   "I didn't mean to upset you"   slyness of marriage when you do and
don't

        group of lesbians amble off   to gay bar   where we get carded
  I produce a WI DL   2 have no id   *these are my kids*   *please*
helpless against the state   tomorrow is International Women's
                   Day and I summon to mind
           the best feminist minds I have known
  ring the door bell of the others   leaving an olive branch in my burnt rubber
if you could learn one thing from me   work on your
persona   Judah sent me a link to the Wikipedia page   "chopped
         liver"   human capital   not well understood
gift economy misinterpreted   the question "do you do this full time"
leaves me crestfallen   "Okay Houston
          we've had a problem here"   what Spacelog actually says

   Monday morning   Laura mutes the Bangles song   it's "just too sad"
Prince of Wales tea comforts me after the pro bono consultant leaves   the bad news
multi-tasking does not = productivity   deadweight
        loss   damn
        hole in the wall   office   supply

on 10th has the brightly colored notebooks   with smooth paper   which I'm hoarding
  but being able to imagine a detailed future drives me

will require many lists

        functional levels of masochism

        I was made

* * *

kindergartners are walking up and down   my block again

holding a knotted rope   after the coldest February on record

since 1934   merely above 40   provides a mental holiday

    "Artists Protest Carl Andre Retrospective..."

     remembering Ana Mendieta

     hectic day

text to Anne :: going to be late

auto-corrected text to me :: uptake a breath   wish Theresa Cha was still alive

      and Mia Zapata   and Mark Lombardi too

   under what circumstances

did my ancestors get here   response :: under strata

of fat and wool   work till you drop ethos   my nephew says he only eats to live

    a ghostly matter   whereby we exchange a knowing look   I

dream   an athletic shoe made for those charged with

     jogging with archaic   responsibility

      lots of deep knee bends lunges   this choreographer had

        powerful

        thighs

* * *

I learn through the machinery   my friends are lonely
            lately my body has been responding   to the environment
                  3 generations of Poles and Sicilians   folk dancing   make
fish chowder   internal metronome   starts slow   ends chugging   like there's no
            tomorrow   walk dog to the canal   see an old woman enter her apartment
                  tchotchkes in the window   everything goes scrambled eggs   part of me
follows her in and inhales mildew   my dog and I are here to keep you company   you
see   in this fantasy   I am company   I play cards   and work part-time   in the
neighborhood   it's one of the most polluted bodies of water   the dog pulls me there
            tries to break through the yellow tape   no boy no!   today is March 14
I'm looking for   Klara   a mysterious data keeper   working for
            Find A Grave   says she was put in the ground
                  on this day   in 1933   opening a portal for my
                                    queer grief

* * *

another thing
know your space
                        only thing I wrote down at Carolee
            Schneemann's   performance lecture   is
"saturated field of color"   she   entering through the back   pushed in a wheelchair
            wrapped in crumpled paper   ringing a bell

I don't turn away from Treasure
with his eye out of socket

Kristin is here   don't see other poets   but Carolee is speaking poet
someone asks a question using the word "painterly"   it was a miserable
walk across the island in a blizzard   Kristin   in the elevator
said now is the time
of the return
of the repressed
it makes sense   makes you miss Mercury
retrograde

it's true   you have to become your own historian   after I "came out"
I got a woman's symbol   tattooed on my shoulder   a woman's body like da Vinci's
Vitruvian Man feet mounted on the plank of the symbol   even proportions have a
canon   whereas I once had regret

now having been subtracted   I consider expanding
into forearm   neck   chest   "to whom do I owe the symbols
of my survival?" (Lorde)

it's true   you have to become the historian of your people
is there someone here to record this?   will there be a recording?
somebody should get this down   otherwise no one   will believe it!

hey poets!
it's the first day of spring

remember when you could hammer nails into the walls
of St. Mark's?

* * *

been waking up at 4:30am
in solidarity insomnia with god knows
how many friends   since learning of a culprit solar storm
messing with our rhythms   thought it was stress waking me   one thought
at the ready   "enjoyment is lost from our labor   I am a fragment..."   (Mayer)
not
explosions on the sun   for moon
children   sweet mundane
dream   look!   two unbroken umbrellas   in the closet   for earth
the dream of form   rather than form itself   the wish for communication
keeps the silence between us   Rukeyser at the Poetry Center   in 1955
speaks of work that comes out of the sources
even
the negative sources
of what we know   "I myself have found
how small a language there is for process
for work and development in its own rhythms   not time as

a series of points   but as plants grow   as animals grow   as people grow   working in
language   keeping very near to the terms of process and doing that consciously"

* * *

watching the footage
of the explosion the dog
howls with the sirens
and I finally really do
cry   even a little   feels
indulgent   but for our avenue
and its dwellers   path from
my desk where I stood up and said
"something bad just happened"
to the balcony of St. Mark's
to St. Mark's Place   meshing with
this footage giving me
a longer take   when people ran
South   this shows what... *that* they
were running toward   not from
and the 3 minutes that it poured
rain   and we decided to wait
you can see people open
and close their umbrellas

* * *

I know where my mom was when JFK was
killed   in typing class   I tell Grey   at my favorite dive   on the block where the
hardware and grocery store   used to be   you can feel the development   in the arches
of your feet   the walls are red   graffiti
and star decals   a nautical theme $3 ale   it's not the only cold
case   I don't know where my mom was
when Pasolini was killed   but I'll say she was   sleeping
given the time difference   a bunch of British guys are playing
Big Buck Hunter   I have a hankering for those big jugs   of Carlo Rossi
with snails   "Sicilian sailor" style   but my grandfather was a steel worker   my mom
said she tried to think of a time when he ever did anything
that made her feel bad about herself   and she could not   I can never really
romanticize   the past again   but I do miss landscapes
watch *The Most Violent Year* with earplugs
moving history beyond nightmare   into structures
for the future   from the dedication of Lorde's *Zami*   last week overheard
a guy on the A saying in NYC you could be on fire   and people would just watch   and I
wrote it in my notebook with a check   Kitty Genovese and the syndrome named for her
"I didn't want to get involved" was actually said by a gay man
terrified of the police
but now I have seen something   else   its particulars
not to be erased
and this solves something

* * *

she produced a Christmas ornament hook
from her purse   in a clear plastic box
"I sat on this in December and I think
I have an infection"   my mom quipped she made it a reliquary
the doctor said   this is impossible   you would
have swelling   redness   a fever   and if untreated   you would die

she doesn't understand how they don't see her symptoms   she has
made them so clear for so long   my book *hart island* just came out
same week Izola Curry died at 98   in a state of delusion she stabbed
Martin Luther King at a book signing in Harlem   if her body is not
claimed   the island will be "her final institutional resting place"   my
grandma says I got my talent from her   she just started writing poems
and says   they are better than mine
because people   can understand them

* * *

the voice of Zoltar says   "what are you waiting for
come on over"   then   inaudible   carrying a
small ottoman   around town   white crushed roses
in the crosswalk   and Red Cross   a crane moves silently   in the corner of
my eye   one of the sisters in my favorite café asks
"what am I getting you?"   that syntax

a latte

I think but don't speak

I'm glad you're ok   and overpay   talked to a friend about

Grace Lee Boggs today   who valued her conversations with people so much

she recorded them   I heard this about Paul Blackburn too

conversations   the radio   poetry   a poet

said he remembers when the arguments used to be about the work

meaning poems   the narcissists are wounded   that explosion

was close   but it missed me   and I am left with another book

to celebrate   if I seem distant it is because all

of my resources are marshaled

moving with danger's pulse   talking

to others   learning to listen better   tell my elder   what I'm afraid of

MY POETRY   it knows things!

as I sip mushroom soup

tell therapist   I regret that I cannot

remember   this is what happens when you think

from your amygdala   it does not retain   it survives   so named for

it's almond shape

can you help it?   "I already

have"   oh so that's the sharp pain!   staggering out of the room

at the 51st minute   with roiling cheap humor

* * *

I watch a movie   a lesbian my age   falls in love with her friend's mom
who's visiting   they're ecstatic together   the night
    before she leaves   her birthday   they eat cake   go to bed together
the older woman catches her train   and has an aneurysm   joy
        so unsustainable   the lesbionic
        disruption   to the older straight
        woman's life   so great
    there can be no integration   she can't even   get home to unpack

* * *

I had received a mysterious email saying   "your water will be turned
off for a few hours tomorrow   please confirm receipt"

"THE WATER IS HOT"

what?

I get the coffee!   a book!   Monteverdi!

    the   water   is   hot

Thank you to Matt Longabucco for reading this manuscript more than once over the years. And thank you to the editors of the following journals who published excerpts from *A Year From Today*.

6X6
Volt
Elderly
Notes: On Administration
Napalm Health Spa — Anne Waldman Issue
seventeen seconds: a journal of poetry and poetics
February: An Anthology
Bone Bouquet
Sinister Wisdom
The Felt
Chicago Review
The Brooklyn Rail
Positive Magnets

STACY SZYMASZEK is the author of *Journal of Ugly Sites & Other Journals*, *hart island*, *Emptied of All Ships*, *Hyperglossia*, and many chapbooks. She has worked at Woodland Pattern Book Center in Milwaukee, WI and was the Director of The Poetry Project at St. Mark's Church in New York City from 2007 to 2018.

NIGHTBOAT BOOKS

Nightboat Books, a nonprofit organization, seeks to develop audiences for writers whose work resists convention and transcends boundaries. We publish books rich with poignancy, intelligence, and risk. Please visit our website, www.nightboat.org, to learn about our titles and how you can support our future publications.

The following individuals have supported the publication of this book. We thank them for their generosity and commitment to the mission of Nightboat Books:

Elizabeth Motika
Benjamin Taylor

In addition, this book has been made possible, in part, by grants from the National Endowment for the Arts and the New York State Council on the Arts Literature Program.